Richard Impey is Bishop's Adviser for Parish Development in the Diocese of Sheffield. He has served as an ordained priest in parishes in Birmingham, Blackpool, Norwich and south Yorkshire, and has been Director of Training in the dioceses of Bath and Wells, and Norwich. He is currently studying for a doctorate in practical theology at Chester University. He is married to Tricia who is also an Anglican priest. They have four children and seven grandchildren.

HOW TO DEVELOP YOUR LOCAL CHURCH

Working with the wisdom of the congregation

RICHARD IMPEY

First published in Great Britain in 2010

Society for Promoting Christian Knowledge
36 Causton Street
London SW1P 4ST
www.spckpublishing.co.uk

British Library Cataloguing-in-Publication Data
A catalogue record for this book is available from the British Library

ISBN 978–0–281–06143–3

1 3 5 7 9 10 8 6 4 2

Typeset by Graphicraft Ltd, Hong Kong
Printed in Great Britain by MPG

Produced on paper from sustainable forests

Contents

Illustrations

Figures

Tables

Preface

In an important sense I think I have been a theologian all my life – and in that same important sense I think many other people have been too. Whether we have been good or wise theologians is another matter, but most people are inevitably engaged in theology in some way, and unavoidably so when we involve ourselves in the life of a local church.

That conviction is my starting point and my theme, for I want in this book to help my fellow theologians to discover the practical theological wisdom that is already present in the congregations that make up local churches, and having discovered it, to join in the shared work of becoming wiser still.

For this reason my thanks are directed first to the congregations of ordinary theologians and saints who have shaped me and allowed me to play a part in their shaping over the years: St Saviour's, Raynes Park; St Mary's, Fetcham; St Martin's-in-the-Bullring, Birmingham; St Cuthbert's, Wells; St John's, Blackpool; St Francis, Chapin, South Carolina; St Mary Magdalene, Norwich; the Kings Beck Parishes in North Norfolk; St Barnabas and St Bartholomew, Heigham; Holy Trinity, Wentworth; and St Mary's, Ecclesfield.

Of course there have also been a number of universities, a good number of books, good friends, colleagues and excellent teachers to whom I also owe a debt of gratitude. To attempt to name them all would be a very long task indeed and so I excuse myself from it.

But the one person to whom I owe more than any other is Tricia, my wife, fellow theologian, companion on the pilgrimage and my tutor in love. To her I dedicate this book.

I am also especially grateful to the staff at SPCK for all their help and encouragement in what is for me the new adventure of writing a book: to Rebecca Mulhearn for the initial invitation; to Steve Gove for his diligence in making my original manuscript much more intelligible; and to Rima Devereaux for her guidance.

Introduction

Asking what people really think

This book is about developing the local church in ways that are appropriate to its own unique character and context. There are many challenges facing local churches today which question whether we should change the way we do things. A good number of people are sure we need to change and are convinced they know both the direction change should take and the way it should happen. I have no basic quarrel with such an approach, but mine is different. I suggest that the kind of change that will produce wholesome development is a shared responsibility of the congregation. We discover the nature of the development we need as we ask ourselves serious questions about the practical wisdom that already guides and shapes who we are and how we do things. Put another way, development begins with questions rather than answers, and the questions are addressed to us as members together of local churches.

What is a local church? The body of Christ

I use the term 'local church' in the ordinary sense of the church people go to, either regularly, or for special occasions like baptisms, weddings and funerals. I am not particularly referring to the worldwide Church or the Roman Catholic Church or the Anglican Communion or the Methodist Church, except that all these are made up of many local churches. A local church usually consists of three elements: a building, an ordained minister or priest, and a congregation. And at the heart of the local church is the congregation, a gathering of people who meet to worship God and express their Christian faith. The church can survive if necessary without the first two, but the congregation is essential.

It is surprising how often this fact is overlooked. There are lots of books about priesthood and the ordained ministry and quite a number about church buildings, but relatively few about congregations, about the people who together make up local churches. Yet it is the local church that is the body of Christ. 'Christ is like a single body with its many limbs and organs, which, many as they are, together make up one body; for in the one Spirit we were all brought into one body by baptism . . . Now you are Christ's body, and each of you a limb or organ of it' (1 Corinthians 12.12, 13a, 27; echoed in Ephesians 4.12; 5.30; Colossians 1.18).

When St Paul wrote this he cannot have been referring to church buildings or clergy; he must have meant all the ordinary believers, what we now call the congregation. It is they – or we – who are the body of Christ. By that image he seems to have meant that we are now the visible, tangible presence of Jesus Christ in the world, for each other and for other people. Unless we embody the Christian good news, other people will not discover its riches and importance. The invitation to become and remain a Christian is an invitation to be part of the body of Christ, which usually means a member of a local church.

What is development? Building up our common life

Development for a local church will mean different things for different churches. Much depends on your starting point. It may well be that a recent change provides the stimulus for development: the arrival of a new minister, a significant decline in membership, a financial crisis or even a substantial bequest. Development is not simply a matter of numerical growth. It is much more about the kind of change which builds up the church. In Ephesians 4, for example, St Paul speaks about how 'each of us has been given a special gift' (v. 7) in order 'to equip God's people for work in his service, for the building up of the body of Christ' (v. 12), which involves unity and maturity. Development may take any number of forms, but its goal will always be building up the body of Christ.

As we respond to this high calling to be the body of Christ in and for the world, we realize that our life together will take some organizing. Indeed it is already being organized, one way or another. Each local church has its own unique way of doing things, just as each family has its own traditions about practical, everyday matters such as how the kitchen is used or how children should be brought up. Much of this book is designed to help us understand how we deal with such practical matters in our own local church. It is based on the conviction that we will only be able to build up the church effectively when we take the trouble to analyse these subtle and at first sight mundane features of how we organize our life together as Christians. At the heart of the matter lies taking the trouble to ask the people most involved what they do, and how and why they do it. This is also to respect them and take them seriously, which in turn is part of the love we as Christians owe one another.

Bothering to ask

I came across this parable years ago:

> John and Mary had been going out together for so long that everyone assumed they would get married. But John and Mary decided

that they were not really suited for one another and announced that they were going their separate ways when they discovered that Mary was pregnant.

John did not think he should marry Mary just because she was pregnant, but he thought Mary would think that.

Mary did not think she should marry John just because she was pregnant, but she thought John would think that.

Mary's parents didn't think they should marry just because Mary was pregnant, but they thought John's parents would think that.

John's parents didn't think they should marry just because Mary was pregnant, but they thought Mary's parents would think that.

You can see the way the story is going! John and Mary end up doing something nobody thought should happen because everyone acted on their assumptions about what other people thought, *without bothering to ask*.

My fear is that we have too many people who know just what local churches need but who *have not bothered to ask* the people most concerned. The only excuse for this is because they have not known how to ask. The rationale of this book is that it not only shows how some of these important questions can be asked, but relies on the members of the congregation to provide the answers, and then engage with the work of building up the body of Christ in the light of what they have discovered.

Practical wisdom

What I therefore want to draw on in the course of this book is what I might call the congregation's practical wisdom. When we become more aware of how we do things, we become more aware of the nature of our shared wisdom as revealed in our practice. Very much like common sense, our shared wisdom seems self-evident, the obvious way to behave. Our practice is for the most part natural to us: we don't spend a lot of time thinking about it; we just get on and do it. But when we do think about it we soon recognize that other people do not always share our practices, just as they do not share our common sense.

Think, for example, about how different people use a kitchen. There are some who restore the place to apple-pie order after every use; there are others who think there are far more interesting and urgent things to do than to wash and tidy up, so they leave it all until last thing at night or until there is not a clean cup left. Both practices work, but they don't work well together. The two practical wisdoms clash. Who is to say which is best? Arguments can be summoned in favour of each: it might be considered best to keep everything clean and in order so things are available as soon as you need them, or it might be better to do menial things at the end of the day when you are tired, and save the hours when you have energy for the more important tasks of life. The advocates of both wisdoms will have words to describe each other's practice – slovenly, unhygienic, lazy; or fussy, wasting precious time, even paranoid.

This clash of practical wisdoms can happen when people come to marry or live together. Unresolved, it will be a permanent source of irritation: one partner is likely to do all the washing and tidying up, the other may well think that he or she is deliberately being made to feel guilty, never being allowed to perform household duties at the time that he or she prefers. Resolving the clash involves recognition of each other's different practices, and a negotiation to find a new pattern of practice which is satisfactory to both. It may be a trade-off: one does everything in the kitchen, the other does everything in the garden. It may be a change in both parties' behaviour: we agree to stack the dirty things tidily and clear away properly every night, possibly discovering that it provides a valuable opportunity to tell each other how the day has gone as we do it.

This may seem from outside to be a relatively trivial example. But if you are trapped inside it, it can be acutely painful. Many couples have had blazing rows about matters like this. Perhaps surprisingly, a good row may be a necessary step toward finding a solution, for it reveals the emotional content of the way we naturally do things. We discover we have a commitment to our practice. We are not likely to change our practical wisdom without good reasons, emotional reasons as well as rational ones. A good reason for changing our practical wisdom – for something still wiser – is that we love one another. This is not romantic love; it is straightforward, sensible, wise love, the agape of the New Testament.

In the same way a local church has its own practical wisdom. It will not be the wisdom of the ordained minister, or of any particular person. Rather it will be the shared wisdom of the congregation, of everyone involved, and it will be rich and complex, made up of all sorts of things – including especially habits moulded by the successes and failures of the church's story. It will be how we do things together. But it may not be as wise as it might be; indeed it is likely not to be, because nearly everyone and every organization will allow that there is room for improvement. However wise we are, the challenge to become wiser still is not an insult (unless we already think we know everything). So you will find that this is not a sharply critical book, exposing the failings of congregations. Rather it sets out to help you – together preferably – discover your practical wisdom and to ask yourselves how that precious wisdom can become wiser. Only in that sense is it about the development of the local church.

What kind of practical wisdom will we be looking at? I have chosen six kinds to work with:

- the wisdom enshrined in the story of the local church
- the wisdom associated with the size of the church and how that might be changing
- the wisdom involved in balancing the implicit purposes of the church
- the wisdom reflected in the church's outlook on life
- the wisdom implied in the stage it has reached in a suggested life cycle for congregations
- the reasons why people choose and value a particular church, and the wisdom for development that this suggests.

The book is divided into two parts of different lengths. The first is designed to help local churches become more aware of their own practical wisdom by reflecting on a number of broad themes. Each of the first six chapters is dedicated to examining one of the above aspects of your church's practical wisdom, while the seventh draws together some other elements not covered within these six themes. The second part consists of two chapters which expand on the practicalities of working with the wisdom of the congregation.

Three perspectives

In summarizing the analytical processes carried out in this book I shall look at what the congregation has discovered via three contrasting perspectives.

Holding up a mirror

One of the most useful ways of considering the process of self-discovery is to think of it as looking in a series of mirrors. Most of us, if we look in a mirror, sense that something needs attention – we straighten our ties or change the necklace for one that better matches our dress. Similarly, when things have been done in the same way for long enough it is easy to assume that this is the natural and right way of doing them; as we become aware of what we are taking for granted, we also become aware that there may be other ways of doing things which could be an improvement. This is something we shall try to understand throughout the course of this book. These symbolic reflections offer a useful summary of who we are and the way we do things, while also providing a quick method of making comparisons between congregations.

These reflections also draw attention to the importance of self-awareness in our common life as a congregation. When we look in a mirror, it is we ourselves who see our reflection; it is not a description provided by anyone else.

Taking a health check

A second metaphor is that of a health check. In this way the exercises for the congregation suggested in this book can be likened to a medical examination. Such an examination may confirm that, as far as we can tell, all is well. On the other hand, it may identify certain undefined sensations or pains as symptoms of a particular illness, a problem for which some treatment is advisable. And if something is wrong, the sooner it is diagnosed and treated the better. At least that is the most straightforward response, though it is surprising how often both individuals and local churches are reluctant to take the steps which promise to improve things. We shall try to understand this reluctance as well.

Drawing up plans

A third metaphor is to think of the local church as a building, which from an architect's point of view needs plans and elevations and specifications to describe it adequately. The information we learn about the congregation can be thought of in terms of such plans. When an architect designs a building the builder needs all this information if he or she is to be able to construct something which corresponds to the ideas expressed in the drawings. Or, to bring the metaphor closer to our purpose, if we are going to reorder or redesign the local church we have to know with some precision what is already there. Part of the value of this way of looking at ourselves is to recognize the significant role of good design and careful planning.

Who is this book for?

This is a book of *practical* theology, and the *practice* is essential. The book will be most valuable when it is read and worked with collectively by local church members, for it will help you understand your common life a great deal better when used in this way. It contains a number of practical exercises, which will be invaluable in helping you discover your congregation's shared wisdom. In particular you will discover more clearly what you are good at, how you are likely to flourish and which particular aspects of your shared life need attention. If, for example, you happen to be looking to appoint a new minister, this will enable you to provide a comprehensive account of who you are as a congregation, and ask prospective ministers relevant questions.

One discovery that you may make if you are able to study this book as a congregation is that it raises questions which are not easy for an individual member to raise in case it appears that a personal criticism is being made. What for you might seem a delicate matter of personal relationships can be seen as a common predicament for many local churches.

I should also say about the process at this point that it is usually both demanding and great fun! You will, I hope, initially find it very interesting to look at yourselves in this way, draw the symbolic reflections you see in the mirror and begin to put your practical wisdom into words. Later, as you get further into it, the process can become more difficult. This will be because the work you have done will push you up against challenges that need facing, hard decisions to be made. I can however encourage you in two ways. First, the challenges and choices you face will be those which *you* have identified (you won't be responding to something an outsider is urging you to do); and second, those choices are likely to be life-giving, transformative ones.

A workbook is available

I have produced a simple *Workbook for Developing the Local Church* which presents the practical work proposed here in a more access-ible form. It focuses on the metaphor of the mirrors, and results in the production of a series of 'reflections in the mirror' which summarize a great deal of the congregation's character. The work-book is ideally supported and explained by the much fuller discus-sions available here. It is published by 4 M Publications and available through <www.4mpublications.co.uk>.

If on the other hand you are reading this book as an ordained minister or other local church leader, I hope you will see its potential as a basis for developing better mutual understanding between yourself and the congregation as a whole. In particular, if the exercises are presented as a programme such as 'Training the New Minister', it will be a valuable way for clergy and others recently appointed to a post to improve mutual understanding. And if you have responsibility for making church appointments and structural changes (such as the combining of con-gregations), it may help to reveal to you some of the complex dimen-sions involved in the process, and suggest useful preparatory work that you might want to initiate.

However, I hesitate to recommend this book for close study by people preparing for ordination or leadership roles in local churches. This is because it is essentially about *congregations and the shared ministry of the local church*. There is no way you can discover a church's shared ministry without the cooperation of a particular local church, for this is the only form in which it exists. I would like students to be aware of the book, of course, and to think of it as a valuable resource when they come to play their part in a local church. But please don't think that the value of what is offered here can be judged by examination of the text alone. In that respect the book essentially forms a piece of practical theology, designed to be tested and assessed in local churches rather than in classrooms, studies or learned journals.

A note on language: One drawback with the simple English word 'you' is that it is not immediately clear whether an individual or a community is being addressed. In many languages this difference between the singular and plural 'you' is built into the very language itself, something we used to enjoy with the difference between Thou and You or even Ye, but which now feels very old-fashioned when used in modern English. Most of the New Testament passages which address us directly use 'you' in the plural; and when I use 'you' in this book I am trying to speak to you as a congregation, as a community of Christians, rather than to you as an individual.

A note on prayer

Building up the body of Christ, developing the local church, will also involve prayer. How to pray together for guidance in these things can be a tricky matter. On one hand, a short prayer at the beginning and end of planning meetings can seem to be little more than a nod in God's direction. On the other hand, the allocation of longer time to open prayer together can unwittingly encourage some folk to use their prayers as advocacy for their own preferred solutions.

How do we expect God to answer sincere prayers for guidance? This is also a question to ponder together. My suggested answer is that God will guide us as we pray *and* as we seek to develop our shared wisdom *and* make careful decisions together. There is no absolute guarantee that our decisions will be right every time, but with prayer every decision can also lead to a deepening of our wisdom.

Building up the body of Christ is not something we do all by ourselves as a result of careful thinking and imaginative experiment: it will be a gift from God. The mysterious and wonderful relationship between God's gracious giving and our faithful receiving is part of what we explore as we pray. Different Christian traditions will have their own pattern of praying for the development and well-being of the church, including for their own local church. I would like to encourage this prayer for the development of the local church, and so I have ended each chapter with a brief prayer of my own. These prayers are written in a meditative style, continuing the conversation which we have with ourselves, with God and with the issues raised in the book. They are not prayers of intercession which can readily be included in typical Sunday worship, but they may be prayed and pondered in small discussion groups or by members of congregations who together are working through the challenges presented by each chapter.

★★★

Lord, we have to admit the church today isn't what it used to be.
We know some churches seem to be growing and doing all sorts
　of wonderful things,
but many more are struggling.
How should we pray for the development of our church?
There are so many things we could include in our prayers
(though it can make praying seem a bit like compiling a
　shopping list)
We would like more people and more money and a better spirit
　of tolerance and encouragement; that would be a lovely start.

Can we hope that this book might show us how to do that?
Looking in the mirror seems simple enough
and health checks are always a sensible idea
while thinking of ourselves as a building that may need re-designing
　is,
well, we will have to wait and see what that really means.
But the wisdom bit should be no trouble:
we have so much experience,
we already score highly there!

Part 1

DISCOVERING OUR PRACTICAL WISDOM

1

Our story

Discovering and interpreting our identity

Our story is a very significant and precious thing. It is part of the way each of us shares with others who we are. It is part of our identity; it's not just a tale told for amusement, it is part of us. Most of us are careful how we tell our stories, and much depends on who we are telling the story to. There are people we trust and love, and we are prepared to tell them things which we would not tell to someone we thought was untrustworthy, or who obviously disliked us. One of the first things to recognize about our stories is that they depend on the listener, the reader, as much as on the storyteller. Or, more accurately, they depend on the mutual relationship between the storyteller and the listener. When we tell someone something particularly personal about ourselves we are also telling that person that we have come to trust him or her.

The larger story will give people we trust an idea of our values and priorities, the kind of choices we make, the sort of things we do and the sort we are hardly likely to do, the kind of things that make us laugh and the kind that upset us or make us angry. It is an indicator of our practical wisdom, that peculiar bundle of habits and convictions which make us who we are.

There are always little stories within the larger story, and these are often illuminating. They can be typical stories, illustrating the sort of things we do:

'He nearly always works late – never leaves the office on time.'
'Whenever she hears of someone ill she'll make them a cake.'

Or they may be unexpected stories, revealing a different side of a person:

'She does wonderful embroidery.'
'He was a cowboy once, you know!'

The really painful parts of an individual's story are not told, though they are often guessed at:

3

'She would have loved to have married him.'
'He had set his heart on becoming a bishop.'

A shared story, such as a family's story, is also significant and precious, and in many ways it is like an individual's story. It will be shaped and edited by the listener as well as the teller. The larger story will indicate values and assumptions. It might be said of one family, 'They have always lived in Rotherham, wouldn't dream of living anywhere else,' while another family has members scattered round the world.

Within the family circle there may well be embarrassing stories about members which we treasure because they make us laugh, but these are not told to strangers. Or there are stories we do tell, but not if one particular person is present, because we know it upsets them.

Then there are the typical stories:

'Every year for as long as we can remember, the whole family has rented a big house by the seaside for a week's holiday.'
'Granny never forgets a birthday.'

There are the unexpected:

'He was a teddy boy when I met him!'

And the ones that are known about, but not told:

'We never *ever* mention Arthur.'

The church's story

When it comes to the story of your local church, similar things apply. It will be shaped by both listeners and tellers. There may be embarrassing stories about members, or stories we do not tell if one particular person is present. There will be a generally accepted larger story:

'We work very hard to maintain the traditions of the village.'
'The church has declined with the economic decline of the neighbourhood.'
'This place has really come to life since the new lady minister arrived.'

And associated typical stories:

'We have an annual music festival to raise money for the renovation of our famous organ.'
'Since the two department stores closed, things have gone downhill – there just isn't the money around these days.'

'The new minister has gone out of her way to draw in the families with young children.'

And there will be unexpected aspects too. One village church has capital assets of almost a million pounds; at another there is an annual tradition of throwing buns from the church tower!

Just like individuals' and families' stories, the church's larger story will express our values and priorities, the choices we make, the sort of things we do and the sort we are hardly likely to do, the kind of things that please us and the kind that upset us. It is an indicator of the church's practical wisdom.

Rival versions of the same story

But one important difference between shared stories, such as those of the church, and most individuals' stories, is the rival interpretation of events. Individuals telling their stories naturally present happenings with an interpretation they can accept. Happenings within a community or family, on the other hand, are often open to a number of different interpretations. For example, at one church the sale of the minister's house twenty years ago is still recounted in quite contrasting ways. One version tells of how the denominational authorities, anxious to get their hands on some easy money, sold the house and moved the minister into a poky little place unable to contain the church office, the meetings of the church council and the Sunday School in the way the old one did. Another version tells of how much more comfortable the minister was living in a more modestly sized house where the children could feel at home without being constantly invaded by church members, a house which was also much more economic to run.

Rival stories like this also serve as rallying cries for different groups. Those who want to preserve as much of the old ways as possible – and who suspect the denominational authorities of ill will toward them – will retell the first version; those who feel that large prestigious houses are not at all what the modern church needs will prefer the second.

You may well find that there are alternative versions of important stories in your own church history.

Telling our own story

The time line

How can we begin to collect the stories which characterize our church life? A simple but very useful starting point is a time line. It's best to start with the period of time that people can actually remember. Ideally, the way to do this is at a meeting arranged for the purpose, at which you ask people simply to mark on a line divided into years the date at which they joined the church. The result will look something like Figure 1.1.

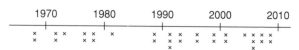

Figure 1.1 Time line showing when people joined your church

Some time lines are long, in the sense that memories go back for 60 or more years. Other churches have much shorter time lines; perhaps no one present has been a member for more than 20 years. The long time line probably indicates a settled community, while the short time line might simply belong to a new church, or it may be a sign of the transitory population in the area – for various reasons people generally move on from here.

There may also be gaps and clusters in the time line. Do they have a straightforward explanation? Perhaps a new housing estate was built nearby 20 years ago. Did the church undertake an evangelistic mission? Was a certain minister rather unpopular?

You can learn something more about yourselves by asking those who are members of the church council (or whatever the church decision-making body is called) to mark themselves again on the time line with a ring or in a different colour (see Figure 1.2). The resulting pattern may reveal that the majority of council members are drawn from those who have been with you the longest, or it may have a much more even spread. What, if anything, does this say about you and how you do things? You could expand the information on the time line by asking everyone who attends church over a sequence of Sundays to complete a card giving the date of their arrival and stating whether they are a member of the council, so that you get as full a picture as possible.

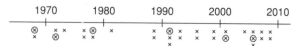

Figure 1.2 Distribution of church leaders along the time line

Collecting the memories

The next stage is to start collecting memories about the church. If you do this at a meeting, I suggest you divide into small groups of people who joined at approximately the same time. The members of each group are then invited to write down any events, incidents, and so on they especially remember. Encourage everyone to say how events or decisions were received (for example, was a particular event welcomed or resented?). Include a question about what they think the church is especially good at.

Alternatively, the information can be collected over a sequence of Sundays, inviting people to write down their memories. Or you could set up a small team of interviewers to collect the information, the stories and the opinions, and then write them up, at the very least, as a series of notes. If you have the time and energy, you could make a much more comprehensive time line, arranging some of the memories and stories by the appropriate year, either on a series of display boards or around the walls of the church, or more compactly through the pages of a booklet. There are almost certainly photographs you could add too.

Using the time line to engage with the wider local community

Your time line material can be turned into a very imaginative display or exhibition, something you can invite the general public to come and see by publicizing it through the local press and radio. When my local church did this we had visits from men who were choirboys fifty years ago, couples who were married here (we had the old registers out, so they could look themselves up). People met people they hadn't seen for years. We included items from the past including ration books, gas masks, telephones with dials and copies of old newspapers. The local schoolchildren came and had a chance to talk to some of us who had been alive so long ago! It was a very rewarding exercise, one that is especially appropriate for an anniversary, but possible at almost any time.

The shape of our story

One valuable way to increase our self-awareness is to draw the shape of our story, making a simple graph that plots morale against time. This is not meant to be a precise mapping, just a visual representation of the purely subjective impression we have of our story. So the story of a church which has essentially gone through a series of ordinary ups and downs will be represented by a horizontal wavy line; the graph of a church with a golden age in the past will have a high point followed by a downward curve; and that of a church that has experienced some

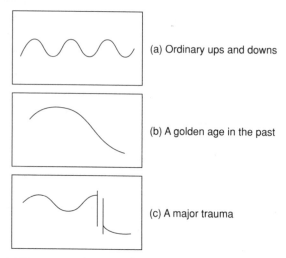

Figure 1.3 The story shapes of different churches

kind of trauma will have either a break or a spike prominent in its line. These are illustrated in Figure 1.3.

Time to reflect

This is probably a good point to pause and reflect on what we have already established about ourselves. We will have:

- a time line showing when current members joined
- an amended time line showing the distribution of council members
- a collection of accounts and stories about what has happened, and what impact some of these events have had
- the beginnings of a list of things we believe we are good at, things which characterize us and describe who we are
- an attempt to draw the shape of our larger story.

Almost everyone will have learned things they didn't know before, and some will want to reflect on possible implications, and maybe ask further questions. If painful stories have emerged we may need an occasion to express the hurt and look for healing. Whatever we have found, it would be good to offer it to God in prayer and worship.

A bundle of stories

The more closely we look at our shared story the more we will recognize that it is really a whole bundle of stories, a collection of incidents, decisions and reactions which live on in our memories and play a large part in influencing who we are, and how we behave. The things we are yet to discover about our size, purpose and so on will also play a part in shaping our self-awareness, so that a fuller discussion of how we respond to these stories will be postponed until the later chapters of this book. But we can already make a number of observations:

- Most stories change their importance with time. For example, the disaster of the church roof being badly damaged in a severe storm turned out to be a blessing in disguise, bringing us much closer together and giving us a goal to work for.
- Some stories take the form of innuendo, hinting at something dark and unknown. 'You remember when the organist suddenly left? There was more to that than we were ever told, you know.' (But they are not going to tell you what it was because they don't know themselves.) This kind of story can be due to malice, but it is often aggravated by a policy of secrecy.
- A few stories take the form of historic legends preserving animosities which ought to have been overcome years ago. We could never cooperate with a neighbouring community 'because they didn't warn us the Vikings were coming!' (This proverbial excuse is still quoted in parts of East Anglia; you can only judge the degree of seriousness from the context, and not always then!)
- Some stories are about acts of generosity and forgiveness. 'When Keith pleaded guilty to stealing from his work, out of his own pocket our rector repaid the firm everything that had been taken.' 'The unmarried church secretary tendered her resignation when it became obvious she was pregnant. The senior warden responded by saying "I think it's probably right that we accept her resignation, but I propose that we ask her to stay on until we can find someone who is perfect in everything!"'
- Some stories are symbolic of our importance. 'We were on television's *Songs of Praise* twice in three years!' 'The new mayor always comes to us for the Civic Service every year.'

Psalm 44 shows how stories can change with time

A biblical example of a story that has changed with time is provided by Psalm 44. The first three verses look back to happy times (at least for the Israelites):

> We have heard for ourselves, God,
> our forefathers have told us
> what deeds you did in their time,
> all your hand accomplished in days of old.
> To plant them in the land, you drove out the nations;
> to settle them, you laid waste the inhabitants.
> It was not our fathers' swords that won them the land,
> nor did their strong arm give them victory,
> but your right hand and your arm
> and the light of your presence; such was your favour to them.

But now (v. 9 onwards) things have changed:

> Yet you have rejected and humbled us
> and no longer lead our armies to battle.
> You have forced us to retreat before the foe,
> and our enemies have plundered us at will.
> You have given us up to be slaughtered like sheep . . .

This abandonment by God is a bitter mystery. The Israelites cannot think what they have done to deserve it, nor can they imagine what advantage it might bring to God (v. 12):

> You sold your people for next to nothing
> and had no profit from the sale

The misery and pointlessness of it all leads to a bold prayer which most of us would hesitate to utter (v. 23):

> Rouse yourself, Lord; why do you sleep?
> Awake! Do not reject us for ever.

though the final verse is a prayer that will not seem too audacious (v. 26):

> Arise and come to our aid;
> for your love's sake deliver us.

There is much to ponder in the way we respond to our story if it moves from success and happiness to suffering and pointlessness. The psalmist looks for an explanation, but cannot find one which makes sense, so he moves into prayer, the kind of prayer which does not hide the frustration and bitterness he feels. The faith of congregations as well as the faith of individuals often has to face bewilderment and despair, and similarly moves not to an explanation but to prayer, crying to God for deliverance.

Our stories and Bible stories

We will return to the theme of our church stories in Chapters 8 and 9. By then we will have collected other perspectives on who we are and how we do things. But it is worth noting that our stories can frequently be set alongside biblical stories in a way that illuminates both. This is one of the best and most fruitful ways of doing theology. It is a method that everyone can join in with, and though it doesn't necessarily produce agreement, it often gets near to the heart of the matter. Take the story of the pregnant church secretary mentioned above. Some people will want to set it alongside John 8.1–11, the story of Jesus' challenge to those who wanted to stone to death a woman caught in the act of adultery. If most members of the church agree with the senior warden they will feel they are acting out a gospel of acceptance, and like Jesus, not condemning her. Other people may feel uneasy; their thoughts may turn to 1 Corinthians 5, a chapter in which Paul deals

Learning from mistakes or just a defensive reaction?

Learning from our mistakes can be harder than it sounds. I think of one local church who would not agree to the minister having secretarial assistance because his predecessor had brought scandal on the church by having an affair with his secretary. Their reaction to the serious failure of one minister was to suspect all ministers. This may be an understandable initial reaction, but if it hardens into a sustained response it will tend to be self-defeating. This kind of learning takes time and patience, and the establishment of trust.

After another church's treasurer was suspected of helping himself to some of the church's money (the accounts were in such a mess that it wasn't really clear what had happened), the church restricted any handling of money to people *who could be trusted* rather than set up clear procedures to ensure honesty by always having two people to check each other. This reaction focuses on the importance of trust, but fails to recognize the importance of clear and transparent procedures, in this case best practice in the handling of money. A very helpful distinction can be made between reactions and responses; an understandable reaction is not always a wise response in the longer term. We often need to review decisions made as reactions to situations to see whether they are sustainable responses.

firmly with questions of sexual immorality in the Church, suggesting that because 'A little leaven leavens all the dough' (v. 6) it is important to 'have nothing to do with any so-called Christian who leads an immoral life' (v. 11). They will disagree with the senior warden and want to see evidence of a firmer discipline. Whichever way the church goes, the theology is in *what they do*, it is embodied in their action. What actually happens reveals their theology, which in this case is their understanding of how God, through his church, deals with people.

Responding to stories at a deep level

Part of the wonderful complexity of stories is how a simple account of something that has happened can go to the heart of who we are. You will almost certainly have felt yourself drawn to one of the above biblical passages rather than the other. In the same way, if you were a member of the church concerned, you would be likely to feel more at home or more uneasy according to the way the secretary was treated. This is part of the very significant unspoken way in which we communicate pastoral care and the gospel to one another. If I, or someone close to me, has been in a similar situation to the church secretary, the way she is treated will be enormously important to me. If she is accepted and forgiven, I will feel accepted; if she is condemned I will feel rejected too. But suppose I have been a strong disciplinarian with members of my own family and brought them back into line, my reactions are likely to be the other way round. I will not see acceptance and forgiveness but rather weakness and indulgence; what others call condemnation I will see as firm discipline. The way we respond to a church's story will be closely related to whether or not we feel a sense of belonging to that church, a subject explored in more detail in Chapter 6.

Summary

Let's now summarize the theme of this chapter using the three perspectives referred to in the Introduction.

The **mirrors** will have shown us a collection of reflections gathered around

- the time lines
- the stories of what has happened, how people have reacted and the things we feel we are good at
- the shape of our story.

Even as we have collected these we will have recognized the possibility of telling the story in a different way (of seeing things differently) and perhaps looking more deeply into the areas which we feel to be our strengths.

The results of the **health check** will depend on what we have found. For example, the time lines may have revealed that the vast majority of the leadership (including council members) are drawn from those who have been around longest and newcomers are – perhaps quite unconsciously – kept at arm's length. We might ask ourselves whether this is a healthy state of affairs.

Perhaps more difficult is when the shape of our story shows a clear decline of morale in recent years, due either to an unresolved trauma or to a golden age in the past. Such a local church can be mildly or seriously depressed. Subsequent chapters may point to deeper reasons which contribute to such conditions, so it is premature at this stage to suggest a treatment.

Some churches are wounded, which is rather different from being unhealthy, though after a while the two conditions can come to look alike. But the treatment of wounds involves forgiveness, reconciliation and repentance, and administering the medicine of these graces is not at all a simple matter. Serious wounds – like those inflicted by a major rift or gross misconduct by senior members – need careful and skilled ministry. In some cases I think that an interim minister can be very helpful, rather than hoping to return to normality as soon as possible.

Looking at our story as a set of **building plans** suggests it is something that we are constantly redesigning, in the sense that we are constantly writing it, and constantly able to rewrite it. We do this not in the sense of denying that certain events ever took place, but in the sense that the way we see their significance changes. A great deal of redemptive history is the rewriting of what has happened. We return to this theme in the concluding chapters, but for the moment a local church whose story is dominated by the feeling that they have been hard done by or badly treated, need to review the way such an interpretation of their story restricts their future.

Our story is probably the one thing above all which holds together the manifold insights, convictions and practices which make up our **practical wisdom**. The relation of our story to our practical wisdom will be a major theme of the concluding chapters.

★★★

Our Father in heaven
so much has happened in this church; it's hard to know where to
  begin.

Perhaps we ought to start with the sins and failures:
there have been one or two really serious matters which still rever-
  berate today –
the disappearance of all that money,
the misbehaviour of one of the ministers,
the things we try not to talk about if we can help it.

Then there have been those other failures:
when the Junior Church leader resigned because we didn't want
  the noise of the children spoiling the service,
the row between the choir and the minister about modern
  hymns,
the failure to raise the level of our giving.

But then we have been hard pressed.
We don't think other churches appreciate how difficult it has been
  for us:
the unexpected death of two real stalwarts,
the expense of repairing the roof,
and the way we are all getting older.

Of course there have been wonderful people and wonderful
  moments:
when the church had standing room only,
when we won the Best Kept Churchyard three years running,
  and
when seventeen youngsters were all confirmed together.

And we are still very good at welcoming people,
we really are very friendly.
The music is excellent and the minister preaches a good sermon.

How do we reflect on all this?
Are you speaking to us through our story, Lord?
Have we developed habits of pride or complacency or self-pity?
Do we look back too much and long for a past glory that is most
  unlikely to return?
Or are we hoping for a miracle? (That would save us a lot of
  work!)
Are we telling our story truthfully?
Is it all too easy to blame other people, social trends, or modern
  life for bringing us to this point?
Have you, Lord God, had a hand in bringing us to this point?

Your kingdom come, your will be done,
on earth – in our church –
as it is in heaven.

Forgive us our sins
as we forgive those who sin against us.

Could we pray, Lord, to see ourselves as you see us?

2

Numbers make a difference

Changing size is not straightforward

The number of people who belong to a local church makes a lot of difference to what that church can do. It is clear that large churches can offer many more activities than a small church can. But the relationship with size is quite subtle, and needs careful understanding.

Our size frequently affects our confidence and general morale. This is often a relative matter: if our numbers are now smaller than they were a year or two ago, we are inclined to become despondent; if numbers are growing then that is taken as an encouraging sign. But our numerical size relative to the size of our church building is also significant. One hundred people gathered for worship in a building designed to seat a thousand has a quite different feel from the same hundred in a building that hasn't quite enough seats for them all.

Our size also relates importantly to the way we organize our common life. By this I mean the expectations we have of one another, especially of ordained ministers, the way we communicate, the range of activities we offer, indeed our whole pattern of working together. This pattern becomes a habit, a set of practical things we take for granted without realizing that our particular pattern relates very closely to our particular size. Broadly speaking there is an organizational structure appropriate to our size; if we change size that structure becomes inappropriate. It is either not able to sustain the larger numbers involved, or it cannot be sustained itself by fewer people.

Such things makes changing size more demanding than may at first sight appear. Churches do change size for a variety of reasons – new housing, the success of a mission or other outreach project, the sense of vitality brought about by a new minister, or the loss of members through death or moving away. But individuals also move churches, and can find themselves delighted or disappointed and often perplexed by the difference between the old church and the new, principally due to the difference in size.

Local churches that do not seem to be changing in size may recognize as a result of working through this chapter together that they neverthe-less have a significant turnover of people (for example, ten join while ten leave each year). This may indicate a kind of glass ceiling to their potential for growth, something which deserves attention.

How big are we?

It is not always easy to decide in terms of numbers quite what size a particular church is. Who do we count? I suggest that we do not attempt to work with precise figures but with generally agreed estimates of the number of people who attend worship regularly, and try to come up with a range. So, for example, we might agree that on a poor Sunday about 45 people attend our church and on a good day about 80. That is quite accurate enough for the purposes of this chapter.

It should be noted that the size of the congregation is not necessarily an indication of the workload of the local church. The location and appearance of one church can mean a large number of weddings, baptisms and funerals when compared with another local church with the same size congregation. That will always be an important difference to take into account, but we are focusing on size, not workload, at the moment.

The four main sizes of church

You will find that your church fits somewhere on a range of four main sizes, which I call small, medium, large and extra large, rather as if they were pullovers. A small congregation has up to about 30 members, a medium between 50 and 120, a large over 180 and an extra large more than 500. Notice the gaps between the sizes. Pullovers of course stretch a bit, but it can be uncomfortable being too big for a medium one and too small for a large. By analogy I shall suggest that it can be

---

The source of these ideas in American thinkers

The American practical theologians Arlin Rothauge and Roy Oswald in the 1980s and 1990s were among the first people to draw attention to the differing characteristics of different size churches, referring to them as Family, Pastoral, Program and Corporate churches. Malcolm Grundy, in *Understanding Congregations*, provides a good account of their thinking. I have worked with these ideas for several years and changed both the labels and the sizes, but not the basic insights, in a way that seems to me to fit the British scene better.

uncomfortable for a local church when it finds itself between sizes. But first, let us look more closely at the characteristics of each size.

The small church

There are a large number of small churches, and they are to be found in all sorts of places. We expect to find them in villages and smaller communities, but they also exist in large conurbations and city centres.

The main characteristic of a small congregation is that it functions very much like a family. There is nearly always a key person, a kind of parent figure who tends to organize most of what happens – maybe because that person has been there longer than everyone else, or has that kind of personality. But most of the organization is informal and tasks are distributed to people as they arise. There may be various folk who normally do things – giving the books out, sweeping the porch or reading a lesson – but if those people are missing almost anyone can step in and take their place.

Small churches do not often have an ordained minister of their own; they are usually served by a minister who is based somewhere else or who has ministerial responsibility for several small churches, or even by a rota of visiting ministers. So ministers are often more like welcome visitors than regular members, and this is one reason why the role of the key person is so significant. It is easy to become involved in a small church if you are willing and prepared to accept the implicit authority of the key person. It is hard to join if you seriously disagree with the key person, who, for better or worse, tends to embody the wisdom of the congregation.

Small churches obviously have limited resources and do not attempt to do many of the things which larger churches take for granted, like having a choir or music group, or publishing a magazine or a website. And roles are not often formal: Joan does most of the visiting 'because she is lovely like that', rather than because the bishop has licensed her as a pastoral worker. Small churches are usually all too aware of their vulnerability. Their members worry about being closed down or taken over or being unable to maintain the church building.

If you are a member of a small church you may want to argue with some of the points I have made, and you could probably add to the list of characteristics. But the most important point about a small church in the context of this chapter is that it tends to organize itself in informal ways, very much as a family does, under the presiding role of a key parent figure.

The medium-size church

By contrast, a medium-size church will tend to focus on its ordained minister. Such a church is likely to have several key people, but they are presided over by the minister, and everyone's relationship with the minister is a key feature of the church's life. This is why such churches are often referred to as pastoral churches, because the personal relationship with the pastor is valued highly by most of the members. Medium-size churches are big enough to do things, small enough to know everyone. This combination of intimacy and scope is an essential benefit of their size.

The medium-size church is likely to organize itself around the minister, in a semi-formal way. Much will depend on the habits and preferences of the particular minister: a few are highly organized and have everything planned down to the last detail, while some leave everything to the last minute. Most, I think, are somewhere in between, and are glad to share responsibilities with other people who may be part of a recognized team. But the minister will know about and be involved in most of the church's activities. There may be teams set up for different purposes – pastoral care, leading worship in residential homes, children's work, Christian Aid Week, Stewardship Renewal, and so on – but if the minister is not directly involved, he or she expects to be kept closely informed about what is happening and what is planned. A medium-size church is the ideal place for clergy who love to be hands-on, but if this size of congregation is located in a parish which also has a heavy workload of weddings, funerals and baptisms it can be an extremely busy place, where it is easy for key people (not just ministers) to become overloaded and in danger of burnout.

If you are a medium-size church you may well feel very possessive of your minister (assuming you are happy with him!) and resent it if he is asked to take on wider church responsibilities. You may see this as taking the minister away from his proper work.

The large church

A large congregation cannot be sustained without a reasonable degree of efficient organization. This may take several forms, but it will certainly involve more work than the ordained minister can do in addition to her other ministerial duties. The chief minister (large churches often have more than one minister) cannot be hands-on; she has to see that the work is done, which is quite different from doing it herself. Such churches will have a church office, staffed by at least one full-time secretary or church administrator. Most of the work will be subdivided and entrusted to responsible leaders, usually with their own teams, overseen and supported by a central team led by the chief minister.

If you are a large church, you may well like your minister to be prominently involved in the wider church or world because it is further evidence of your importance.

Part of the attraction of a large church is the sense of life and activity, of important things going on. Nobody can take part in every event, but the choice of activities to participate in is evidence of vitality. But in order not to lose the fellowship which is an important element of what churches have to offer, most large churches have small home or cell groups to which everyone is invited to belong. These usually focus on prayer, Bible study and mutual support, but may also set themselves specific evangelistic or social tasks. In this way most people belong to a large church on at least two levels – to the small cell and to the large gathering, both significant aspects of the church.

> *Large churches involve a lot of people*
>
> There may not be very many large and extra large churches, but they do involve a lot of people. For example, in 2005, in the four Church of England deaneries of Sheffield, 2,547 people attended just five large churches while 4,011 attended the remaining 55 parish churches on the Sunday when the usual Sunday attendance was counted. This means that nearly 40 per cent of worshippers attended large or extra large churches while the remaining 60 per cent attended small or medium-size ones. (Reliable figures for more recent years are unfortunately not available.)

The extra large church

Needless to say, extra large churches are usually extremely well organized and everything is highly professional, with many full- or part-time paid staff. The extra large church has many of the characteristics of the large church, like cell groups for example, but it often has a greater sense of its own power and significance. This can make it difficult for the extra large church to relate easily to neighbouring churches or central bodies like the diocese or circuit or union (or for these to relate easily to the extra large church). Extra large churches usually have sufficient resources (people first, but also money) to perform many functions, and because they are efficient and effective, can usually work much more quickly than a whole number of smaller churches attempting to work and make decisions together. And just because of their efficiency they tend to be impatient of what they see – often with some justification –

as the inefficiency of some smaller churches. By the same token, they can also be very generous in their support (with people and money) of struggling churches, especially those which share their own convictions and priorities.

Size and mutual dependence

As the size of a local church increases from small to extra large, so its dependency on other churches decreases. Most small churches could not survive without the support of other churches (mediated through some central body), while most extra large churches are more than self-sufficient and could, for most purposes, make a unilateral declaration of independence. The power aspect of the size of a local church is not something that I want to pursue further at the moment, but it remains an important feature.

The size of congregations in the New Testament

Jesus preached to crowds of thousands, yet he also promised to be there when two or three gathered in his name. Numbers, as such, do not seem to have interested Jesus. Paul, on the other hand, seemed anxious to present the gospel to as many people as possible. We do not have any firm evidence about the size of the churches Paul founded; the fact that they met for the most part in people's houses suggests that the numbers were small to medium (otherwise they would not have fitted into the houses whose size is described by archaeologists). We would love to know what happened to the three thousand who were added to the believers in one day, and the others, presumably hundreds at least, who soon joined them (Acts 2.41). Did they try to meet all at once at the temple? If so, did they form a distinctive group with prayers of their own or was their worship more or less the same as that of the other faithful Jews around them? Did they scatter after the martyrdom of Stephen and form smaller groups, and if so how big were these? So far as I have been able to discover, questions like these cannot be answered with anything more than conjecture.

Changing size

Having established these primary characteristics of different size local churches, as summarized in Table 2.1 overleaf, I want to move on to discuss some of the issues involved when we change from one size of congregation to another. This happens in one of two ways: (1) when individuals move from one church to another of a different size; and (2) when a congregation itself either grows or shrinks in size.

Table 2.1 The four main sizes of church

Small	Medium	Large	Extra large
up to 30	50–120	over 180	over 500
Functions informally, like a family	Focuses on the minister; some delegation	A more formal structure to the organization with tasks subdivided	A professional organization with distinct departments

Bringing our wisdom with us

Whenever we move from one congregation to another we tend to bring with us the practical wisdom which has served us well in previous situations. We naturally assume that we will continue to do things in the new place in the same way that we did them in the old one. But often this assumption needs careful examination, because what is appropriate for one size of church may not be right for another. Of course there are usually numerous other factors involved. The churchmanship is likely to be different, as is the style of worship, especially music, and the church building will be different too – but for the moment we are focusing on size.

Some people stay in the same local church all their lives, but many move several times. Typically some move to the seaside or the country on retirement and find themselves in smaller local churches than they have been used to. Smaller churches do less than larger ones, so this kind of move can be a disappointment; we miss the liveliness and the buzz of the bigger church. We might think it will bring some fresh life to the community if we donate a new hymn book or start a home group, but if we do so we may find ourselves frozen out. Unless we persuade the key person first, our helpful suggestions may well be interpreted as a takeover bid!

The experience of clergy

People who expect to change congregations several times include ordained ministers. Those who have been trained by placements or curacies in larger churches frequently find themselves being asked to minister in small local churches for their first sole charge. This makes sense at one level (probably there will not be such overwhelming responsibility and work), but it runs the risk of placing clergy in local churches which organize themselves and whose size-related ethos is quite unfamiliar to the new minister. If such clergy expect to relate to their small churches in the same way that they saw the ministers who trained them relating to larger churches, they are likely to be disappointed in the response. And if clergy are disappointed in their congregations, the congregations are likely to be disappointed in turn, and a downward spiral can begin.

But going to a larger size church may not be any easier. Jesus certainly suggests in the parable of the talents that those who show themselves responsible in little things will be given greater responsibility (Matthew 25.21, 23), but clergy who have proved excellent ministers in smaller churches and are 'rewarded' with a larger, more prestigious church sometimes find themselves unable to cope, because the good way they used to do things is not now appropriate. This will be especially true for those who love to be hands-on. I do not want to suggest that it is always unwise to make such changes, only that it is unwise to make them without careful thought and supportive training.

Discovering your experience of different size churches

As a congregation you can discover quite a lot about yourselves and your experiences of different size churches by doing a simple exercise together (as illustrated in principle in Figure 2.1). Using four columns to represent the four main sizes of church, invite each person to draw a small circle in the column of the church size where they had their first experience of church, and a small square in the size they now find themselves. They should then join the two with a simple line. Those who have belonged to several congregations may want to indicate this with several small circles, numbered in sequence, or you may prefer to

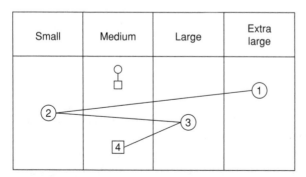

Figure 2.1 Grid indicating members' experience of changing church size

simplify this to show only the first and last. Clergy in particular may decide that the size of church where they had their formative experience of ordained ministry might be preferable to their first in chronological order. Everyone should include the size of church where they had their longest or happiest or most significant experience of church, especially if that is now in the past. The result of this exercise can be quite illuminating.

Figure 2.2 illustrates a medium-size church where only one of the members has had experience of large or extra large churches, while Figure 2.3 shows a similar medium-size church where more than half have had experience of larger churches.

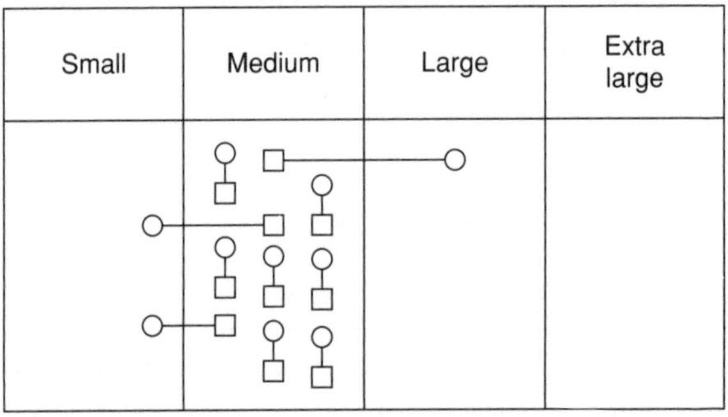

Figure 2.2 Medium-size church where only one member has had experience of a larger church

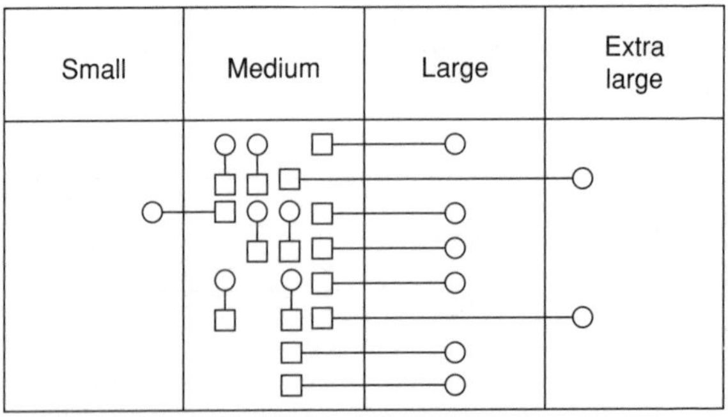

Figure 2.3 Medium-size church where several members have had experience of larger churches

At a personal level you might invite individuals to reflect on whether changing size was for them an encouraging or a disappointing experience, or one which they hardly noticed. Some people may have felt cramped and restricted in smaller churches, so a move to a larger church was liberating; others may have felt that downsizing to a smaller church was like coming home to a place where they were noticed and valued. Experiences will differ.

At the level of the congregation as a whole, the main difference between the churches in Figures 2.2 and 2.3 is that there are a substantial number of people in the second who have experience of a larger church, and who may be presumed to have brought with them a certain familiarity with, even 'knowhow' about, how larger churches work. This might indicate that it should be easier for the second church to grow into a large church than for the first, where there is no one with substantial experience of a church of any other size. On the other hand it is possible that many of those with experience of larger churches actively prefer the nature of a smaller church and would resist growth in size.

Becoming a different church

In fact local churches often find it very difficult to make size transitions. There are two interconnected reasons for this. One is simply that old habits die hard. The other is the realization, often at an unconscious level, that to change size *is to become a different kind of church*.

Old habits here refer to the way a particular size of church organizes itself. The medium-size church, for example, in which everyone values their personal relationship with the minister – and the minister values it too – can only grow into a large church by letting this valued feature go, and developing a more formal structure where members do not have ready access to the minister but instead are referred to other people who are authorized to deal with whatever is needed. This is usually achieved by setting up a church office, staffed by a secretary or parish administrator, with different teams to deal with different areas of church life, something which may be seen as a way of making the minister more remote and harder to get at. There is some truth in this accusation – but the change is made in order that the church as a whole, including the minister, can relate to more people. The old habits, especially when they are especially venerable and remain unchallenged by people who have a memory of different habits (as in the church represented in Figure 2.2), also seem the right and proper way to be church; we do not know any other way.

Put like this it may sound like a lame excuse. Unrecognized, it can function as a powerful obstacle to growth in size. Recognized, it points to a real choice: do we grow by changing size, or should we plant another medium-size church, and try to grow that way?

Some churches have actually chosen to grow by multiplying medium-size congregations, rather than by becoming a single large church.

A different kind of church

As we have seen, a different size church is also in important ways a different kind of church, and so to change size means losses as well as gains which all the members will notice. As a useful exercise, I would encourage you to draw up a table (see Table 2.2) contrasting what your own size church presently offers with the possibilities of the size it might become or aspire to. Ask yourselves, for example, about what you expect from the different size churches – what you expect as a member, what you expect from the clergy, how people share information (communications), who does the administrative work and where, and so on.

Table 2.2 Comparing the ways different size churches organize themselves

	Smaller churches	Larger churches
What are the advantages of the different sizes?		
What are their natural limitations?		
What do ordinary members tend to expect?		
What expectations are placed on clergy?		
What expectations are placed on other leaders?		
How do people best communicate?		
How and what do these size churches communicate to outsiders?		
Where does day-to-day administration happen and who does it?		
Any other contrasts?		

Your own answers to such questions will be important, especially if you are confronting the challenge of a size transition. If that is the case it is very helpful to look into what is involved in some detail, but here I can only offer some general observations.

For many clergy – though not all – in churches growing in size there is a difficult transition to be made between doing things yourself and being responsible for seeing that things are done (usually by other people). It lies at the heart of good management, but there are several reasons why many churches find such good management difficult:

- Clergy and lay people tend to share a pattern of expectations, which is that the clergy themselves will be the best people to do most things; they will be best at leading worship, at preaching, at pastoral care, at chairing committees, for they are the professionals; they have been trained to perform these tasks. (This view is often tenaciously held, even when all the evidence points against it.)
- It is often perceived that recruiting, training and supporting other people to do such tasks is harder work than doing it yourself.
- Many church members have a bias against anything that sounds like management, as if it were all manipulative, rather than seeing that the way that a church organizes its common life is worthy of careful reflection.
- On the other hand, in a hierarchical church – and church traditions which lack the obvious hierarchy of bishops can still have a hierarchy of prestige attached to certain offices and churches – this transition is also about promotion and career development, sometimes called preferment.

The tensions involved in this transition between doing things yourself and being responsible for seeing that they are done are experienced in teaching and the medical profession as well. Most head teachers cannot do much actual teaching; and senior nurses can spend more time organizing other nurses than they do working face to face with patients. In the case of the local church, however, the shared management of transition can make the process less problematic for all concerned.

The church under stress

One symptom of the need to make a size transition is stress (though not all stress is a symptom of the need to make a size transition!). Everyone feels that there is too much to do and feels in danger of becoming overwhelmed, unable to cope. This happens whether you are growing larger or becoming smaller. It is a matter of matching tasks and resources. When you are becoming smaller you find you haven't got the resources – people, energy, money, time – to keep doing everything you used to do; you are becoming overloaded. In order for the church to survive without totally collapsing, some tasks (things you have come to feel are a vital and normal part of being a church) have to go. Deciding what to keep and what to let go is a task most of us are reluctant to face, but unless decisions are made, or made for us, increased stress is the likely outcome.

When you are becoming larger, in contrast, you may find that the organizational structure which served the smaller church cannot cope with the larger numbers who now attend. The children's team who could manage with 20 youngsters cannot cope with 40; the minister who used to answer all phone calls and emails personally cannot do that when the phone rings 20 times a day. There's no real mystery here, just a challenge to the way we organize our local church life together. Many churches are reluctant to become more businesslike if this means establishing a church office with an administrator and various members of staff and volunteers, each taking full responsibility for different aspects of the church's life. This is partly because it promises to cost a lot more and partly because it seems to move us in the direction of a faceless efficiency. (Many of us have a touching affection for amateurism and for making do in a voluntary organization like the local church.) To make such a transition involves a revision of our instincts and preferences as well as a structural reorganization.

Ministry teams

Many local churches have shared the tasks traditionally carried out by the minister by developing ministry teams. This is usually a very good way of working together, but each church will find that the nature of the ministry team will need to be appropriate to its size. What follows are some suggested ways of approaching this challenge, according to the size of your church. Although an oversimplification, I hope they may prompt valuable discussion:

- A ministry team in a small congregation should involve everybody, at least in the sense of everyone who is willing to be involved.
- In a medium-size church the ministry team members will usually relate directly to the ordained minister, who frequently directs operations and supplies the tasks or the information (for example, about who is in need of a visit). The team is often a mix of 'authorized' folk and willing volunteers who have the trust of the minister and the congregation. A lot of the work will still have the feel of 'helping the minister', even if this is a way of putting it which many rightly want to question.
- In a large church there will be several distinct teams. The central ministry team is made up of competent people who are themselves leaders of other (satellite) teams engaged together in a particular sphere of church work. The central team members will have responsibility for making most of the decisions relating to their sphere; the minister (or chief minister, if there is more than one) will only be involved if the leader thinks it necessary. The central ministry team is responsible for coordinating the work of ministry and setting priorities; the day-to-day ministry is carried out by the satellite team

members. The central team members include a mix of professionals and volunteers.

- An extra large church will have a multitude of teams. There may even be several teams who share the same basic work, for example, an A and B team for youth work. These are essentially working teams who would normally have one of their members attending a coordinating team as well. The majority of the leaders are professional or semi-professional, part of a structure which offers oversight in the form of care, support and, if need be, discipline. The central team does not – cannot – concern itself with day-to-day matters but concentrates on strategy and external relations.

Summary

Some more aspects of what might be involved in making a size transition will be discussed in Chapters 8 and 9. For the moment let me summarize these reflections on the size of the local church.

The **mirror** simply shows us what size we are at the moment. Identifying our size in this way has the basic function of allowing us to avoid inappropriate comparisons. It doesn't make much sense to compare ourselves with churches of a different size: they will be able to offer things we can't, but we will be able to offer things they are often unable to do. It also prepares us to recognize that our past experience of a particular size church may actually make it difficult – not impossible – to appreciate a new church of a different size. This is something prospective ministers especially ought to ponder. Clergy who love to be hands-on ought to think very hard before accepting an appointment to a large church where they will have to spend much of their time organizing others to do the work they love to do themselves. One advantage of reflecting together as a local church about your size is that all of you are better placed to understand the reasons why certain changes are desirable, and so more likely to enable them to happen.

Churches undergoing a **health check** are most likely to be those which are feeling under stress, and the diagnosis may well indicate that they are in a size transition gap. This may well explain some of the stress they are experiencing, though there may be other explanations too. Stress is not to be taken lightly for it can lead to burnout, not just for clergy but for the lay members of a church as well.

By looking at the **building design** we can see that there are ways of organizing our life together in our local church which are appropriate to our size, as I hope I have made clear already. Attempting to organize ourselves with a 'wrong size structure' is inevitably frustrating and unsatisfactory.

If this is our predicament, we meet it best with a definite policy decision, drawing up plans in order to add more rooms or decide which ones to close off. If we are becoming smaller, we should choose to become a good example of the smaller size church, rather than a poor example of a church struggling to do all it did when it had many more members. If we are growing numerically, we should set about reallocating the space in the building, in other words designing the organizational structure which will be capable of sustaining the larger size before the increasing numbers overwhelm us.

One strand of **practical wisdom** is the way we normally do things. Reflecting on size has enabled us to see that the way we normally do things is probably appropriate for one size, but certainly not for all. So if we are facing a size transition, we need to revise the way we normally do things. The word 'appropriate' becomes an important part of wise vocabulary; the old way, the 'normal' way of doing things, has not suddenly become 'wrong', just inappropriate.

A second strand involves the way we learn things as a community. A congregation working together through this chapter will have gained important shared insights about the relationship of their numerical size to many of the things they do. Being told by a perceptive leader that something is the case is one way, but discovering together that it is the case is rather better. It employs our shared wisdom (which is not identical with the wisdom of any one person). The more people who perceive for themselves the need for any particular change, and who take part in planning it, the easier the change becomes – even when it is not particularly welcome.

A third strand might invite us to reflect on the way we can unwisely confuse size with importance and success. For many churches, 'going for growth' has been an overriding goal. Certainly the complacent church has little to commend it, but larger is not always better, least of all if it comes at the cost of quality.

★★★

We live in a world, Heavenly Father,
where many people see size as a measure of importance and value.
We are urged to 'Go for growth', and that often makes us feel guilty:
Merely holding our own would be enough!

How important is size to you, Lord?

There are a lot of advantages in being small.
We all know each other,
everything is friendly and informal,
we all muck in and it all goes along quite happily.
We have to share our minister with other churches, of course,
but it usually works well.
The minister is there when it's essential,
but otherwise we get on with things ourselves.

The medium-size church has its advantages,
small enough for everyone to know each other but large enough
    to do quite a lot.
We have a modest band of singers,
a small number of regular activities for children,
groups for men and women
and a number of teams doing practical things.
And we have our own minister.
It's true that finance is a problem;
keeping the building in good repair is expensive,
but we have got by so far!

And larger churches can be great too.
There is a special buzz about being part of a successful and
    thriving organization.
So many possible things to support,
real quality and professionalism in the preaching and music,
excellent opportunities to learn and
practical projects which are challenging and exciting.

Of course there are drawbacks as well.
Many of us stretch ourselves to the limit so we really can't take on
    anything more.
More people would mean more work and we are not sure we could
    cope.
What we really need is more workers, more helpers,
but all those sorts of people are already very busy these days,
and it doesn't seem fair to ask them to take on yet more.

We feel a bit trapped, Lord!
Grow in numbers and we would be overstretched,
we don't think we could cope.
But shrinking doesn't help much either,
because it's often the workers who go first,

and anyway you're left feeling a failure.

(We really don't want to join that group which some people call 'Failing Churches'.)

Give us this day our daily bread (including all those things we need to sustain us).

3

The purposes of local churches
Balancing potential rivalries

'Fit for purpose'

In recent years the phrase 'fit for purpose' has come to prominence, most often in a negative sense: someone important will say that this organization or that government department is not fit for purpose. It sounds like a stinging criticism, and is probably meant to be, but to say how organizations are, or become, fit for purpose is not a straightforward matter.

This is particularly true for churches, the purposes of which are hard both to discern and to define. Indeed churches frequently have several distinct purposes at the same time, because their instinct is to embrace and support almost any project which seems good and wholesome and worthwhile. When this happens we can end up being very busy doing all sorts of good things, but probably not doing anything really well. The aim of this chapter is to help you identify the purposes of your church, in order to enable you better to fulfil them.

Clarifying our purposes

In order to try to clarify their purposes many local churches have worked hard at producing a mission statement. This seems like a good idea, but the fate of many carefully crafted statements is to be displayed in the church porch, and on the website, and then for all practical purposes to be ignored. This is not because people are perverse, but because most churches have very broad and imprecise purposes which cannot be captured adequately in a sentence or two. For example, we may want to bring other people, and ourselves, closer to God in Jesus Christ, but because God has made us as human beings with so many different strengths and weaknesses, there are a multitude of possible ways in which this could happen. By contrast, making cars, selling mustard or trying to find a cure for cancer are purposeful activities which are much easier to define and measure.

The purpose of the Church is a central theme of the Christian faith which needs to be explored and clarified in every generation. In this chapter I am going to approach this theme from a practical point of view, by offering a framework for making clear to ourselves the contrasting purposes we take for granted in our church life together. When we have done this we can compare what we have found with what we believe is sound teaching on the matter, whether from Bible or church tradition or both. This way of going about things will seem back to front for many people, but I invite you to try it because I believe it can illuminate many of the tensions which a lot of local churches experience.

A framework for understanding the purposes of the Church

The framework I am suggesting is three-dimensional: imagine a pyramid with a square base and four sides tapering upwards which from a distance would look like a spire, pointing heavenward, pointing to God. We can use this framework to illustrate five main purposes of the Christian Church. The vertical dimension is the Godward purpose of the Church, the offering of worship, prayer and praise. The four sides of the pyramid viewed in the horizontal dimension stand for four purposes which concern God's creation, especially human beings, including ourselves. Each side (purpose) reaches upward, indeed points upward to God in worship, while expressing the purpose of the Church in a distinct way. The four sides represent

1 a church which offers worship and the fellowship of mutual support in the Christian life
2 a church which offers worship and understands itself called to serve the needs of the wider community
3 a church which offers worship and sees its task as necessitating a campaigning stance, a prophetic witness, on a particular issue
4 a church which offers worship and not much else.

A church's purpose embraces both God and other people

You can also see in this framework a representation of Jesus' summary of the law in Matthew 22.37–39: "'Love the Lord your God with all your heart, with all your soul, and with all your mind.' That is the greatest, the first commandment. The second is like it: 'Love your neighbour as yourself.'"

The vertical dimension represents the first commandment, while three of the four sides represent our neighbour. The first side represents the neighbour who worships with us, the second the local neighbour who may not worship with us, but whose need is our concern. The third represents concern for the neighbour who may be physically more distant but whose predicament is such that we feel we must do all we can to change things for the better. (The fourth side doesn't quite fit this scheme; rather it represents the kind of church people want to attend for worship without becoming involved in all the other aspects of church life, as we shall explain shortly.)

No individual church in my experience is a pure example of any one of these purposes. Most combine all four, but in varying proportions. I shall be suggesting that it is in fact the mix of purposes which is most significant, but first let me describe the contrasts between four churches, in each of which one of these purposes dominates.

Worship and fellowship

A church whose dominant purpose is to worship God and to provide a fellowship of mutual support will almost certainly be characterized by frequent meetings and get-togethers in addition to services of worship. An after-church fellowship or coffee hour will be well attended and may last as long as the service itself. The conversation could be wide ranging, but it will include enquiries about others' welfare. It won't be thought of as gossip so much as genuine interest and concern for one another. There will often be a social committee arranging several events throughout the year, and there will be a high degree of mutual pastoral care. This sort of church encourages people to join in and feel that they belong to the local family of God's people. It will practise 'prayer and parties', as Jack Nicholls, a former Bishop of Sheffield, recommends.

Worship and service

In a church where the dominant purpose is to worship God and to serve the needs of the local community there will probably be the same after-church fellowship with wide-ranging conversations, but the bias will be toward the practical matters involved in serving others. Exactly what form this service takes will depend on the local context. It may be basic involvement in activities or clubs for young people and support for the elderly, or it may be more specialized, like a project for the homeless or in support of asylum seekers. At the after-church fellowship you are more likely to be asked whether you can help out with something than to be asked about yourself. This is the sort of church William Temple, a former Archbishop of Canterbury, had in mind when he described the Church as an organization that exists for the benefit of non-members.

Worship and campaigning

A church that is both dominated by worship and takes a clear campaigning stance on a particular issue is not very common in Europe, but some campaigning purpose is usually present in most churches. Many local campaigns have a limited life, especially when they succeed. Other campaigns, like anti-apartheid and civil rights, change character with time and as events unfold. Some, like fair trade and environmental responsibility, are open-ended. It is not easy to generalize because the particular issue shapes the campaign, but this kind of church is usually led by someone who knows a great deal about the issue and is prepared to take every opportunity to bring it to people's attention. Although this is generally not a very dangerous thing to do in the privileged Western world, it is worth reflecting on how many people in other parts of the world risk (and some lose) their lives because they believe that campaigning or standing up for justice in God's name is part of the integrity of a Christian. Archbishops Oscar Romero and Janani Luwum come to mind as Christians who were killed because they insisted on a prophetic witness. We know their names because of their high profile in the Church, but there are many more whose names we do not know.

Worship and not much else

The fourth kind of church is one that provides worship and not much else. People who appreciate this kind of church value the opportunity to worship with others, to sing God's praises and to hear the word and receive the sacraments, but they do not wish to be involved in all the other activities that can go with attending church. At one level this could be described as a consumer's attitude to church; at its best, however, it enables those who live out their Christian values in their work, their family responsibilities and in service to the community to identify with the worshipping community. They do these things as Christians, as salt and light, as Jesus urges us in the Sermon on the Mount (Matthew 5.13–16), but not as one engaged in these things alongside other church members.

Taking a vote

At this point, I suggest you stop reading and take a vote! If you want to become more aware of the purposes your members are pursuing, an excellent way to do so is to undertake the following simple exercise. As soon as the four purposes laid out above have been explained, invite everyone to complete two voting papers of the kind illustrated in Figure 3.1.

Ask each member to distribute ten votes (or points, it doesn't matter what you call them) between the four purposes on each paper to indicate:

- on the first paper, the balance of purposes that person feels applies in the church at the moment
- on the second paper, the balance that person would like to see if things were to change.

Worship + service To provide opportunities for worship and to serve the needs of the wider community		**Worship + fellowship** To provide opportunities for worship and a fellowship of mutual support	
Worship + campaigning To provide opportunities for worship and to take a campaigning stand on a particular issue		**Just worship** To provide opportunities for worship and not much else	

Figure 3.1 Voting slip to indicate the balance of purposes in the church

If you can possibly do this now, it will make the rest of what is to be found in this chapter much more relevant. You can of course make a guess at what the result might be, and you may just be right. But if you are mistaken you will draw all sorts of incorrect conclusions about your local church from what follows. That would be at the very least a waste of time, and might make difficult situations even more difficult. As I suggested in the Introduction, this is a book of *practical* theology, and at this point the *practice* is essential. I want to help you understand a real live local church, not some abstraction. And perhaps even more important, the insight you gain may well help you understand and solve difficult tensions which are not easily discovered and resolved in any other way.

How to express the results

These votes are not about winners and losers; they are about the shared perception of your community about itself.

Simply add up the points given to each purpose, and ask someone whose arithmetic is up to it to express these as percentages. (Most computers will have a program that will do this for you and draw a pie chart of the result as well.) The two sets of results will first allow you to see how people perceive the church at the moment; and second show what people would like it to become. The difference between the two will be a valuable indicator of any pressure for change.

Interpreting the results

There are three broad types of result, but your local church will be like only one of them (except that the pressure for change may suggest you would like to move from one type into another):

1 One of the four purposes receives 50 per cent or more of the points. I call this a 50+ church. This usually indicates a straightforward situation, one in which the 50+ purpose clearly dominates the life of the church. The other three purposes can and do function as minority concerns, and this often works happily, in the sense that of itself it rarely generates conflict. A minority concern does not mean an unimportant concern; in this context it means one that isn't dominant.

2 Two purposes receive approximately equal support, so they are competing for dominance: a 40:40 church. This too can work happily, but it is a potential source of conflict and tension. The tension may arise because the two distinct purposes are in competition for valuable resources – which basically means people – and because they need contrasting organizational structures to support them. (Other factors in such tension will be discussed shortly.)

3 Three purposes receive approximately equal support, a 30:30:30 church. You might think that this could be a bold attempt at balance and comprehensiveness, but unfortunately it more often means frustration. This is because, as in a hung Parliament, no one purpose (or party) has a majority. Whoever puts forward a serious proposal has only 30 per cent of natural support, with the rest either opposed or indifferent to it. It does not matter who puts forward the idea; each party is in the same boat.

It is important to emphasize at this point that I am not saying that 40:40 and 30:30:30 churches are to be *avoided*. Far from it; only that they are more difficult to sustain happily *unless as many people as possible are aware of what is happening.*

Where does your church come in this scheme?

By now you will have discovered where your church is placed according to this typology. It is possible, of course, that you don't fit exactly into any of the three broad types (for example, if the points are 45, 20, 20 and 15), though you will be able to see that you are closer to one category than either of the other two. For most people, looking at a pie chart is a better way of judging this than simply working with percentages.

We have in fact two things to bear in mind at the same time. One is where we think we are, the second is what we would like to become. But before we look more closely at the balance of purposes, I want to stress the Christian nature of each of them, because I don't want to give the impression that one of these purposes is necessarily better, or more Christian, than the other three.

The Christian nature of the four purposes

These four purposes represent four contrasting ways of being a church; all four purposes are Christian, but they challenge each other. Each relates to a different emphasis to be found in Scripture and the traditions of the Church, as well as being more or less appropriate in different historical, geographical and cultural circumstances. Each purpose can be seen as a challenge to the other three, and it is likely that you (like me) will have a preference for one, or at the most, two of them. This can tempt us to un-church, or at least look down on, those whose preferences – or whose callings – are different.

The purpose of fellowship

To stress the importance of fellowship and the mutual support that Christians can give one another is probably the most common form of church purpose. It echoes verses such as Galatians 6.10: 'Therefore, as opportunity offers, let us work for the good of all, especially members of the household of the faith.' It builds on the bonds of affection and commitment which can flourish in a worshipping community. It is the embodiment of that sense of being bound together in Christ, which distinguishes us from all other human beings to whom we are bound by creation and a common humanity. It is a place for many of us of healing and acceptance, of encouragement and love. We belong here; it is like a large family, the family of God's people. Of course it can also be a place of disappointment and frustration, a community that stifles us and cramps our style; it is certainly not a perfect community. It has its treasure, as Paul puts it, in 'earthenware jars' (2 Corinthians 4.7). The Church, as the body of Christ, mediates that gift of fellowship which is for many of us such a valuable part of the gospel.

The purpose of service

But even though we recognize the indispensable role of Christian fellowship there is also a call to serve, to recognize Christ in the hungry and thirsty, the stranger who needs welcoming, the person without adequate clothing, the prisoner. The story Jesus tells of the sheep and goats (Matthew 25.31–46) quite properly unsettles us, implying as it does that a cosy self-centred fellowship cannot be all that Christianity is about. So we are called in ways that are appropriate to our time and place to serve the needs of the wider community. In city centres it may mean doing what we can for the homeless, and the obvious casualties of modern life who gather there. In other places it may involve giving time to help with uniformed youth organizations, with lunch clubs for the elderly, with community involvement of all kinds. Christ calls us to follow him, not just for our own sake but also for the sake of other people. Part of our dignity is that we have gifts to use in service.

The campaigning purpose

For some churches and church leaders, a particular injustice unsettles us so much that it becomes our special calling. The plight of asylum seekers, wanted by no one, excluded by unfair rules and regulations; the plight of women trafficked for sex; the stupidity of waste and pollution poisoning the planet; the evil of political and military power used for the benefit of the wealthy few against the majority; scourges like HIV & AIDS and malaria – the list is long and full of real challenges. How can we be complacent in the face of such evils and injustices? The purpose of the Church must surely include a large place for overcoming evil and working incessantly for peace and justice in the world. This is the role of prophetic witness, raising a voice against complacency and blatant sin.

The worshipping purpose

For other Christians the church is one resource among several; one sphere of activity among many in which they can express their faith. They value the opportunity to worship, to join in the praise of God, to hear the word read and preached, to join in communion at the Lord's Table, to pray with other people. But they find their fellowship in other communities, their work is their service to the wider world and they give generously to charities working for peace and justice. They want to be free simply to attend; if we put pressure on them to become more involved they may well stop coming altogether. Such a use, such a purpose for the church is made possible in many places because of the long history of the close involvement of church and community, especially the involvement of the church in infant baptisms, weddings and funerals. It may seem to some, especially to those who see themselves struggling to keep the church alive, that such people are taking advantage of those who are more committed. That may be so, but some of those people may genuinely be grateful for the gift which more committed generosity makes possible.

Two important points need to be made before we go further. One concerns the basic maintenance of the church community; the second has to do with evangelism.

Viability

Keeping the church community viable is inevitably part of what every church has to do, but this is not its purpose. It can feel like a purpose, especially in difficult times, but the real purposes are deeper: they are the reasons for its existence, the purposes I have listed above as worship, fellowship, service and prophetic witness. These purposes cannot be fulfilled if the church ceases to exist, so keeping the church alive is important – not for its own sake, but for the sake of God's glory in worship, and for the sake of our own human need to share our lives with one another in a constructive and wholesome way.

Evangelism

A number of people challenge my fivefold typology by suggesting that I have forgotten the purpose of evangelism. I would respond by saying that I see the good news as being embodied in the purposes of the Church. Evangelism includes an implicit invitation to join a community of Christians, because the good news is that God invites and accepts our worship, offers us fellowship and encouragement through our fellow believers, calls us to serve the needy and to work in whatever way we can toward the Kingdom of Heaven. I find it hard to understand a gospel that has nothing to do with the Church; indeed I think that it

---

Provoking love

There is a lovely phrase in the epistle to the Hebrews about how we should 'consider one another to provoke unto love and to good works' (10.24, AV). The Greek word which is translated 'provoke' here means to irritate or to exasperate, to prick or spur on; as parents and teachers will often be aware, the child who seems to be the cause of trouble has frequently been provoked – sometimes quite literally pricked – by one of the others who is trying to maintain an air of innocence! I love the idea of mischief being employed in the business of encouraging goodness – so much more fun than the heavier ways of preaching and scolding.

is possible to say that the overriding purpose of the Church is to embody the Christian gospel.

Organizing each purpose

These contrasting characteristics involve contrasting organizational structures. What I want to explain now is that each of these four purposes flourishes best with its own distinctive organizational pattern.

Organizing fellowship

A local church which is dominated by worship and fellowship tends to thrive on the informal spontaneity of many of its members, something that is evident in the worship as well as in the fellowship. Enthusiastic sharing of the peace is often a symptom of this kind of church. Genuine friendship and concern for one another cannot be made available through efficient rotas; you need people who relate well, good listeners, 'people people' as they are often called. So a basic expectation of leaders in this kind of church is that they will be accessible and approachable. Members expect to be drawn in and to belong, which means in part feeling that they count and are noticed. Learning people's names is important, as is having time and opportunity to meet and talk.

Fellowship churches are frequently busy churches holding lots of events such as parties, coffee mornings and discussion groups (plenty of chances to meet and get together). This sort of church is organized by a wide variety of people, offering a choice of ways for members to meet. The orientation is inward, toward one another, though this does not mean that it is necessarily exclusive or unwelcoming. Most relationships are informal and happen spontaneously in such a context. But care for people with particular needs is shared with those who are regarded as better qualified to deal with them, which usually means the clergy and authorized pastoral workers.

Organizing service

A church that focuses on offering worship and serving the needs of the local community, and in particular the needs of non-members, will be organized in a quite different way. Key people at the heart of such a church will need to 'network' with others in the local community to keep in touch with changing needs, and with the provision being made by other bodies. Part of what such ministry can offer can be the facilitation of communication, even a kind of fellowship between the voluntary and statutory bodies engaged in helping. The value that public bodies outside the church place on the interest and concern of churches, especially the concern of clergy and identifiable church leaders, is often very high. There is value in simply keeping in touch and being concerned.

But then local churches of this kind are likely to be active in service in specific ways; exactly how will be related to their context. Some churches have on their doorstep obvious social challenges like homelessness and the presence of asylum seekers; others seek to help those caught up in the problems of family and marriage breakdown; still others set out to help by providing lunch clubs where people, especially those living on their own, can get a good meal and meet others. This kind of activity only thrives when it has competent organizers at its heart, people who are good at seeing the potential others have for helping, who are good at encouraging others to volunteer and who support those others in the work they do, who are good communicators. Essentially these are people who see that things are done – but don't try to do everything themselves.

Sometimes this kind of service requires the leadership of someone with special skills, although often people without specific qualifications can be involved. It should be noted, however, that increasingly government rules and regulations – such as those relating to hygiene and child protection – are setting standards, and requiring qualifications which ordinary folk may not have, though they can acquire them.

The demands of campaigning

The local church which, through the joint activity of its members, takes a campaigning stand on a particular issue often does so in support of a national or international campaign. A coachload of members will travel to national venues to join a protest or make an appeal, as did many participants in the Jubilee 2000 campaign and the anti-war protests of recent years. Other, less dramatic, campaigns are concerned with fair trade or environmental issues (though these campaigns too can include dramatic protests). A few campaigns are local, concerned for example with the building of a supermarket or bail hostel or bypass in the parish. Ordinary support and involvement in such activities requires enthusiasm and persistence. Leadership calls for special knowledge, skills as an advocate and publicist, and a creativity that thinks of new ways of drawing attention to important issues that are easily overlooked because they have become too familiar. The modern prophet needs an office equipped with every kind of communication technology, and staffed by competent people with the political instinct for seizing the smallest opportunity.

'Just worship' requires organizing too

By contrast, a church that offers worship and not much else will almost certainly be rather more formal. The focus will be on worship well led and reverently organized. There are likely to be few additional activities for the congregation and what there are will be more formal, for example, concerts or lectures. Everything that happens will be organized by a small core of people, volunteers as well as professionals, who do this on behalf of the larger number of people who attend. Those who come appreciate what is available, but they do not want to be drawn in. They are happiest relating in a courteous rather than a friendly way. They do not mind if others do not know their names, and they do not go out of their way to learn other people's names.

Patterns of expectation

Each of the above purposes involves different patterns of expectation; in Table 3.1 I have set out some of these differences in general terms. You will find it helps develop your own self-awareness if you try to identify specific examples of things your church does, especially in the row labelled 'Primary evidence'. You may also find it helpful to think hard about any other contrasts that occur to you, and ask whether the contrasts I have suggested ring true in your experience.

Balancing competing purposes

Holding a healthy balance between the four purposes can be demanding and difficult. It is made easier, I believe, if as many members of the local church as possible are aware that it needs to be done, and will only be done well if everyone makes their contribution.

Local churches which lack awareness of their purpose nevertheless occasionally achieve an unconscious harmony. This is probably because they are dominated by one purpose (a 50+ church) and are held together by having their set of expectations met by nearly everyone.

Competing purposes can, however, lead to frustration. Too often local churches which are unaware that they are trying to be 40:40 or 30:30:30 churches are frustrating places, with the adherents of one purpose consciously or unconsciously fighting with the adherents of another. For example, the group responsible for fellowship gatherings believe those who spend a great deal of time helping the homeless ought to lighten up and enjoy themselves occasionally, while their counterparts believe that all the others think about is enjoying themselves, closing their eyes to the needy on the church's doorstep. So we find the tragedy of good people supporting a good purpose fighting other good people supporting a different good purpose. And when you are caught up in this kind of conflict, it's very difficult to think of those who take a different view as 'good'; misguided, perverse, uncooperative are easier words to use, but they are not more helpful. All too often we use a praise–blame,

Table 3.1 Patterns of expectation in churches with different purposes

	Worship + fellowship	Worship + service	Worship + campaigning	Worship and not much else
Expectation of members	belong	be an active helper	support	attend
Expectation of leaders	good mixers	good organizers	well informed, seize opportunities	efficient producers (as in dramatics)
Expectations of clergy	friendly, approachable, sympathetic	good connections in the community	an able advocate, good with media	good preachers, good public persona
Forms of pastoral care	mutual and member directed	directed toward the needy non-member	large scale (in terms of justice), aimed at structures	from clergy when needed
Primary evidence	good worship and active social life	good worship and active involvement in the community	good worship and good publicity for the issue	good worship
Any other contrasts				

Two books have prompted this typology

Where has this way of looking at the purposes of a local church come from?

It has two distinct sources: the first is *Congregations in Conflict* by American sociologist Penny Edgell Becker, published in 1999; the second is Charles Handy's *Understanding Voluntary Organizations*, first published in 1988.

Penny Becker studied about two dozen congregations in three townships near Chicago. She wanted to investigate the nature of conflict within congregations, aware that such conflict is an increasingly common phenomenon. Attending the churches and synagogues, she interviewed many of the members and assembled a great deal of information. She discovered that there did not seem to be any strong correlation between conflict and the church's polity, that is to say whether it belonged to a wider church with a hierarchal authority (usually a bishop), or whether the congregation regarded itself as an independent authority. Rather she distinguished five types of congregation on the basis of the evidence she gathered, each with its own typical patterns of conflict. (Not all conflict is negative of course; many tensions and conflicts are the source of wholesome growth and development.) She named these

- Houses of Worship
- Family Congregations
- Community Congregations
- Leader Congregations
- Mixed Congregations

and described them as cultural models of local religious life. The Mixed Congregation is a mix of the first four and usually experiences the bitterest or most severe forms of conflict.

Charles Handy does not base his book on specific empirical research but describes it as 'an anthology, with some interpretation, of other people's work'. A central theme of his book is that there are three broad types of voluntary activity:

- mutual support
- service delivery
- campaigning.

Each of these 'carries with it an unspoken and implicit assumption about the nature of organizations and how they ought to run' (p. 12). These different assumptions are often a source of organizational conflict.

The four types I have offered in this chapter are not the same as Penny Becker's first four, but they are adaptations of them, shaped strongly by Charles Handy's insight. This has proved a valuable typology for helping local churches recognize that some of the conflicts they are experiencing – but not necessarily all of them – are due to clashes of organizational assumptions, as Handy might say, or to the collision of different cultural models, as Becker might put it. It locates this kind of conflict within the organizational structures of the congregation rather than seeing it as a clash between powerful personalities.

good–bad, win–lose framework to analyse and understand such conflicts, which tends only to aggravate the problem and force us all into entrenched positions.

Identifying conflicts of purpose

If your local church recognizes that it may be in the frustrating predicament of attempting to fulfil purposes which interfere with each other, it is essential to analyse the situation more carefully. A straightforward way of doing this is for as many members of your congregation as possible to make two anonymous lists: the first list should include everything they themselves feel they do as part of the life of the church, and the second everything they see other people doing. As far as possible, *actions* should be listed in preference to *offices*; so, for example, 'count collection', 'bank cash', 'keep accounts', and so on should be listed rather than just 'treasurer'.

From the two separate sets of lists, you should next construct two comprehensive lists by putting all the items in alphabetical order, noting the frequency with which the same words occur; for example, if 'count collection' appears in four people's lists of what they do, the comprehensive list should include 'count collection (×4)'.

This may prove to be quite a long task, and is perhaps best done by a few people working together with the lists each member has provided. Keep any editing to a minimum; sometimes it is obvious that different words have been used to describe the same activity, in which case it makes sense to bring them together, but don't reject any item at this stage.

The length of the lists will indicate just how many actions make up the life of your church, which is also an indication of how complex it is. If you compare the two lists carefully you may discover that there are a number of activities that are 'hidden', or at least 'not noticed': items included on the first list but not on the second. It is worth pondering these; sometimes they may be items most people felt were too trivial or obvious to mention, like 'turning the lights out', but occasionally they may be more significant. The aim is to involve everyone, not just those who perform the obvious duties. The person who 'just' polishes the brass each week can easily be overlooked when compiling such lists; this process helps such people feel noticed and valued.

The next step is to see whether you can allocate the items on the first list to any of the four purposes we have distinguished. This may not prove straightforward, for two reasons. First, many activities serve more than one purpose; for example, running a lunch club will serve the needs of people in the community and, at the same time, encourage fellowship between the church members who staff it. Second, quite a lot of activities belong more naturally to one of two other categories: either they are part of our worship (which in any case is common to each of the four purposes we are working with), or they are part of maintaining the church – the sort of activities, like looking after the money, which are essential if any of the purposes are to be carried out. So I suggest you work with seven rows, as set out in Table 3.2; the first two rows should include all the things that relate either to the provision of worship or to the church's maintenance, both of which are common to each of the four purposes.

Begin by working in small groups of four or five people. Each group should choose, say, 12 (or more or less, according to the time available) of the most significant items, allocating each to what they agree is its

Table 3.2 Allocation of activities to the main purposes of the church

Activities primarily connected with worship

Activities connected with maintaining the church

Activities contributing to the fellowship of mutual support

Activities connected with serving the needs of the wider community

Activities connected with campaigning for a better world, part of our prophetic witness

Activities connected with providing worship (and not much else)
NB This could also include much that is in the first row

Activities that don't fit any of the above categories

most appropriate row or rows – the same item can go under two headings or more if necessary. If the group don't agree about where an item should go, then it should be entered in all the rows the different members think appropriate.

The opinions of all the groups should then be combined by gathering them together in a master table. This will give you a more or less comprehensive picture of how the members see the balance of purposes served by all these activities, together with the evidence.

Such a table will need thoughtful interpretation. The number of items listed under each heading is not necessarily a good guide to its relative importance, or to the time and energy the activities require. Making allowance for this, you will be able to estimate whether your shared initial view about the balance of purposes in your church is endorsed by this more detailed evidence. If you agree together that the first impression is not backed up by the evidence, then you should revise things accordingly. But if there is sufficient agreement – we are dealing here with broad trends, not precise percentages – then you have important evidence of the kind of activities which are likely to be rivals or to interfere with each other unless they are held in a wise balance by everyone.

A further exercise for churches with a potential conflict of purposes

If you are a 40:40 or 30:30:30 church, I suggest you take the specific activities you have now listed under the two or three purposes and repeat the exercise about what each activity needs from members, leaders and clergy, adding some notes about the resources each needs in terms of time, energy, skills and money (and anything else you feel is relevant). This may seem unnecessarily complicated, but it does not take a great deal of time and is well worth doing. You may end up with something that looks rather like Table 3.3 overleaf.

You may choose to focus simply on the two or three purposes which are apparently competing for dominance, or you may wish to include the activities which belong to all the purposes, and include worship and organizational maintenance. The second choice will take longer but provide you with a fuller picture.

The point of doing all this – which may seem very complicated when you read these pages on your own, but which in fact is not so difficult and is usually very interesting when you come to do it together – is that you have a much clearer picture of what is happening in the life of your church.

Table 3.3 Allocation of resources in a 40:40 or 30:30:30 church

	Members' contribution	Leaders' contribution	Clergy's contribution	Resources needed (time, skills, money etc.)
Purpose A				
activity A.1				
activity A.2				
etc.				
Purpose B				
activity B.1				
activity B.2				
etc.				
Purpose C				
activity C.1				
activity C.2				
etc.				
Purpose D				
activity D.1				
activity D.2				
etc.				

Possible ways forward

As a result of these exercises, at least three things may become more consciously part of your common life.

1 You may be able to say to each other, 'I'm glad our church is trying to do purpose A (which is not my priority) *and* purpose B (which is where I feel most at home) because I can see that *both* contribute to the glory of God.' In this way you allow and make space for those activities which are not immediately attractive to you and which do not draw on your talents. You embrace diversity within a generous unity.

2 You may recognize that you – and potentially everyone else – have been given talents which are more happily employed by one purpose than another. In particular it may be clear that it does not make sense to expect everyone to join with equal enthusiasm in everything!

3 An additional task or activity is seen to emerge from this diversity (you may have noted it already), and that is the task of maintaining the balance and therefore the unity of the church. This is the general responsibility of everyone, and the special responsibility of the leadership, including the clergy.

These reflections on the balance of purposes in a local church might alert its members, for example, to the strong possibility that a new minister can unwittingly upset the balance that prevailed before he or she arrived. If the old minister, for example, had a mild bias toward the purpose of worship and fellowship and the new one is slightly biased toward worship and service, the congregation will notice the shift. In a 40:40 church some will be pleased while others are disappointed. If everyone can recognize that such a shift was highly likely it at least enables a more thoughtful response to be negotiated.

Organizational problems in the New Testament churches

Organizational problems are not new. Chapter 6 of Acts reveals the tension that existed in the church between those who spoke Greek and those who spoke Aramaic, the language of the Jewish people of the time. It focused on the daily distribution – from the money held in common (Acts 4.34–35) – which seemed to overlook the Greek-speaking widows. The Twelve said in effect (Acts 6.1–6):

- this is important;
- if we do it (which points to an unspoken assumption), more significant things will be neglected;
- you choose wise and spiritual people to do this, and we will authorize them.

The kind of work the deacons of Acts 6 engaged in is not further reported, which is not surprising since most of us don't say much about cleaning and cooking and other domestic matters, unless they go wrong. Two of the deacons appointed in this way soon became famous for quite different reasons; Stephen as a martyr (Acts 7) and Philip as an evangelist (Acts 8).

Summary

The **mirrors** will have revealed important aspects of what you are taking for granted about the purposes of your church, and how you would like the balance of purposes to change. As I have already stressed, the balance between these legitimate purposes is a key matter, together with the direction and strength of any pressure for change indicated by the difference between the present balance and a desired balance. The first thing to say is that this is only an initial impression, valid enough on the day it was made but not necessarily an indication of the long-term position of the church. Often this look in the mirror represents the very first time a congregation has thought about such matters. The result itself may act as a spur to thinking even more about our purposes, and in doing so, revising them.

Just occasionally I have sensed that some members of a local church have wanted to question the result because it does not fit with their own perceptions of what their particular church is about. By all means question it, but let it also question you. Church leaders in particular sometimes need to recognize that the congregation does not agree wholeheartedly with them, but is reluctant to say so directly. A surprise result – in this mirror and in some of the others – may be a way of communicating this disagreement.

Bear in mind too that the desired balance will need testing before we act upon it. This is not because we are hypocritical in expressing our wishes, but because we may well be wishing for changes which we ourselves cannot immediately provide. By definition the present balance of purposes is made possible by resources we already possess. A desired balance may well require additional resources, which may be difficult to obtain. Many congregations, for example, want to do more to serve the needs of young people in their wider communities, without having the people, the money or the skills to do it.

Looking at our balance of purposes as a **health check** may enable us to understand the sense of frustration we feel, for example, as a result of being what I have called a 30:30:30 church, as well as pointing toward a fruitful way forward. A similar diagnosis may help a 40:40 church understand better the tensions of its predicament.

'Health' is not necessarily the best word in this context, except that if the tensions and frustrations are not addressed, chronic ill-health is a likely outcome. The tensionless church, like the tensionless relationship, does not exist except in a world of complacency and indifference. Tension and frustration are not in themselves unhealthy. The key challenge is to find ways of allowing these tensions to become fruitful rather than destructive.

A key factor in discovering a confusion of purposes or predicament in the way described in this chapter is that most of the people involved have discovered it *together*. Thus it is discovered as a *shared* predicament, and not something that can reasonably be blamed on any single person or group. It is also discovered by people registering their own opinions, and in that sense cannot but be owned by them. It is never a matter of accepting the opinion of a supposed expert. This pedagogical route is vital, because it simultaneously locates the responsibility for action with the congregation as a whole. It calls for a development of the congregation's own *wisdom*.

Considering your **building design** may point to the need to devise an organizational structure which will enable your congregation to meet the challenges of their own complexity in a positive way. You may find that one of the bedrooms is being used as an office for your self-employed business, while the kitchen is full of motorbike parts because the garage is overloaded with gardening equipment.

While a building is a fixed structure, of course, what may well be needed is something more flexible. Every local church will have a constitution and rules of procedure for governing its life. This is most commonly provided by the denomination to which it owes allegiance, though thoroughly independent churches will have their own. Such constitutions and procedures represent the distilled wisdom of earlier generations and should certainly be respected, but they rarely cover every eventuality and tend not to address the predicament of purpose confusion.

The local church's **practical wisdom** in this respect will focus on finding and maintaining a workable balance between the different purposes. This can take several different forms. Smaller churches on the whole tend to thrive when one purpose dominates, but other purposes take turns to feature. The purpose which most commonly dominates in small churches is that of providing worship and the fellowship of mutual support. This is their normal operating mode, so to speak, but from time to time they also serve the needs of the wider community by hosting a village festival or providing a summer holiday club for children, or supporting homeless people in the nearby town with a fundraising effort. A modest contribution to campaigning for particular issues might take the form of a Christian Aid Week event and a Fairtrade stall in church every quarter, and even 'worship and not much else' could be provided for on Back to Church Sunday. The method here is that of focusing on the different purposes in turn.

Larger churches will probably relate to the different purposes through different groups whose primary concern relates to one purpose or another. Each different purpose is more or less permanently catered for. For fellowship there might be a catering committee, a Sunday Lunch Club, a social events organizer; for service a weekly late-night soup run, a volunteer group helping to staff the drop-in centre for young people, a Senior Citizens lunch team, and so on. Here wisdom is needed to manage the rivalry between the various purposes – a natural rivalry which is in competition for resources: people, time, energy, money and attention.

This kind of balance can seem best maintained by strong leadership, but it is also greatly helped when as many people as possible recognize the need for it. This can be especially so when leadership changes, as we have already noted; a new minister can unknowingly upset the balance that has been achieved. When you do achieve a good balance you tend to forget that that is an achievement, and assume it is the natural state of affairs!

A complementary wisdom to this balancing of purposes is that of discerning the gifts, aptitudes and convictions of church members. Some people are happiest behind the scenes, making the tea, so to speak, while others are prepared to be up front and take a lead. Some will be most at home organizing social events; others will be impatient with that and want to be involved in making an impact on the wider world. Helping each other find our vocation within the life of the church (which for most people is not the totality of their vocation) is a shared responsibility of the whole community.

***

'Why?' seems such a simple question!
Why are we a church?
Why do we do the things we do?

Lord, grant us truthfulness as we reflect on our purposes as a church.
Quite a lot of what we do is habit,
we carry on doing what we've been brought up to do.
There is a lot of comfort in the familiar ways,
the historic buildings,
the favourite hymns,
the prayers we know off by heart,
the same seats, and the same faces.

Basically we want to worship you.
We want to *hallow your name*
and pray that *your kingdom may come and your will be done*
On earth as it is in heaven.
We want to acknowledge your place in our lives and our world,
we want to *build up the Body of Christ.*

And so part of our purpose is to build up the fellowship,
to support one another in our faith by listening and understanding,
to provoke one another to love and good works,
to share our faith with our children,
and to encourage others to join us.

Another part of our purpose is to be *salt and light,*
serving some of the needs of the local community,

working alongside other people of good will
as we try to make life better for our neighbours.

And we have a concern for the wider world,
where there is so much injustice and suffering.
We cannot put it all right but we can do something;
we can support fair trade, we can give through the aid agencies,
we can campaign for a better and safer and fairer world.

And perhaps we can make room
for those who only want to join us for worship,
who don't want to get caught up in all our other purposes,
or who may prefer to do these things elsewhere and privately.

And then, as we look more carefully, Lord,
we realize that these good purposes can get in one another's way.
We can build up such a strong and cosy fellowship
that we forget all about the local community and the wider
  world.
Or we can get so caught up in serving the needy
that we neglect our families.
In such ways good people can fall out with other good people
who are serving a different – but equally good – purpose.

Grant us a wise balance,
a responsible and mature choice from among the many possible
  purposes
you hold out before us in your world.
For the kingdom, the power and the glory are yours
Now and for ever. Amen.

4

Our outlook on the world
Not everyone sees things the way we do

The way we see the world is not fixed. It will vary according to where we are and what is happening to us. If we have just fallen in love, or been appointed to the job we had always wanted, or if our church has just completed a successful mission, then the world may seem a wonderful place, and our outlook will be generous and sunny. But if we have just been made redundant, or find ourselves in the midst of messy and protracted divorce proceedings, or if several members of the church have been killed in a car crash, then life itself will feel grim, and our outlook will inevitably be darker. But beneath these obvious contrasts there may be a deeper consistency in our outlook, characterized perhaps by a determination to do our best whatever happens, or by a sense that there is a purpose and meaning in it all, even if for the moment we cannot see what it might be.

Each of us tends to have a preferred outlook, one that comes more or less naturally to us. We may have inherited it or learned it or had it shaped by early experiences; but however we came by it, it is ours. It is the natural attitude of our souls. Some of us regard it as a blessing, or in contrast as something we have to struggle with, while others take it as given. It is almost like a voice within which is regularly giving us one or more messages, such as:

'Go on, you can do it!'
'Be careful, you will probably fail!'
'Life is an adventure, take the risk!'
'Keep your feet on the ground.'

In the background, meanwhile, are other voices, maybe saying,

'You are worthless.'
'You are wonderful.'
'You are a fool.'
'You are great.'

The four basic outlooks

The American theologian James Hopewell developed a comprehensive way of classifying the outlook of people and congregations. He suggested that there are four basic outlooks on the world, which I simplify as follows:

- You can look at the world relying on an authoritative account of how things are. Usually for Christians this is based on the Bible or on church tradition. A congregation with this outlook will tend to ask, Is this in line with Scripture? Is this genuine church teaching? Key words defining this outlook might include obedience, rules, laws. (This is looking north according to the convention I am using.)

- You can look at the world relying on the inspiration of the spirit. Guidance for life tends to come not from an external authority but from an inner voice or conviction which tells you what to do. A congregation with this outlook will expect signs, and will sense God's hand in almost everything that happens. Key words will include inspiration, vision, adventure. There will be a sense that we are called to be a hero in the drama of life. (Looking east.)

- You can look at the world as something that possesses an ultimate unity and harmony. A congregation with this outlook believes in the importance of understanding this harmony. It will emphasize learning and education, reconciliation and peace. Key words will include understanding, education, discovery. (Looking south.)

- You can look at the world relying on what our five senses teach us. A congregation with this outlook will regard itself as essentially practical and down to earth. It may be sceptical about visions and inspiration; it is more likely to be persuaded if the money is already to hand! Key words would include realism, pragmatism, hard facts. (Looking west.)

None of these outlooks is superior to the other three, and each comes into its own in particular but different circumstances.

Reflecting on the four outlooks

Now take a little time to reflect on these contrasting outlooks. One way to do this is to write out the key words against the four directions of the compass (north, east, south and west, as illustrated in Figure 4.1 overleaf). The basic arrangement of the compass is significant; you can look north-east or south-west or even south-south-east, but you cannot look in opposite directions simultaneously.

You may come to recognize that you are more inclined to identify with one or perhaps two outlooks. If you find that difficult, one clue is to identify an outlook you generally reject, because we frequently define ourselves in terms of what we are *not*. The more you *think* about it the harder it can become, but if you are content to go along with your first impressions, your *feelings* about it, you are likely to be able to recognize your own preferred outlook.

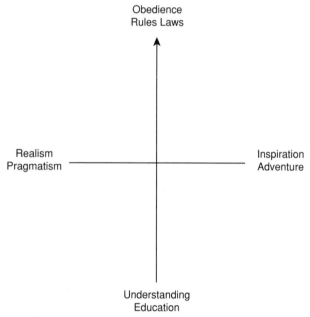

Figure 4.1 The four basic outlooks

No one is suggesting that this outlook needs to be defended or justified by logical arguments; it is just the way you look at the world.

Discovering your shared outlook

The next stage is for everyone in your congregation to indicate their preferred outlook. The simplest way of doing this is to give everyone a slip of paper with the four points of the compass already drawn on it, as in Figure 4.1; each member of the congregation should draw an arrow on the diagram in the direction most closely representing the outlook he or she favours. All these individual arrows are then copied on to a single diagram.

The result of this exercise is usually intriguing! I have carried it out more than 50 times with different congregations, and there has always been a high degree of shared outlooks, amounting to a dominant outlook

James Hopewell

James F. Hopewell was Professor of Religion and the Church in the USA at the time of his death in 1984. He had long studied congregations and was preparing his book, *Congregation: Stories and Structures*, when he died. Edited by Barbara G. Wheeler and published in 1987, it has since become one of the most influential books in the field of congregational studies. Hopewell was convinced that the best way to understand a congregation was to listen carefully to the stories it told about itself. The *narrative* of a church carries a great deal of information about its meaning. He drew on contemporary studies of literature and was particularly influenced by Northrop Frye's book, *Anatomy of Criticism*. This encouraged him to look at the nature and movement of the congregations' different stories, leading to the development of his theory of basic outlooks which I have outlined in a very simplified form. Hopewell went on to relate congregational stories to ancient myths and legends. For example, he saw in one congregation's story distinct echoes of Sleeping Beauty – the congregation was sleeping, waiting for the arrival of the Prince who would kiss it into life. I am not inclined – partly because I am not familiar enough with the literature of myths and legends – to follow Hopewell far down this path. But what he says about a congregation's outlook is very illuminating, as is what he has to say about the symbolic (which I will develop in Chapter 6).

Careful students of Hopewell will recognize that I have rotated the compass points he allocates to the four outlooks. This has no bearing on the relationship between the different outlooks.

for that particular congregation. Another way of putting this is to say that there has never been an even spread of arrows in all directions. The majority of arrows have always been on one side of an imaginary line drawn across the compass face. Typical results are illustrated in Figure 4.2 overleaf.

What does this imply? At one level it may simply confirm that like-minded people tend to associate with one another, and there is perhaps little surprising about that. But if we look more closely we may recognize that the few folk who are looking in markedly different directions may well not feel at home in this particular congregation, for opposite outlooks are seriously at odds with one another.

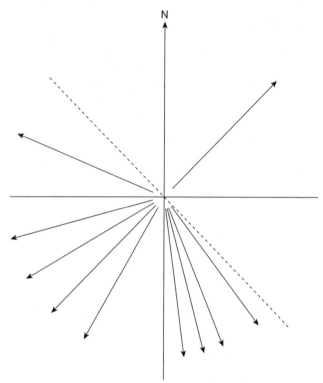

Figure 4.2 A typical distribution of outlooks within a congregation

Contrasting outlooks struggle to work well together

Each outlook is an implicit criticism of the other three, and especially a rejection of the opposite outlook. For Hopewell this lies in reasons I have not so far mentioned and can perhaps best be illustrated by considering the *interpretive movement* that is implicit within each outlook.

The northerly outlook

For the northerly outlook, which emphasizes rules and obedience, the interpretive movement is from an initial unity or harmony through disobedience to some kind of punishment or tragic consequence. The interpretation of the story of Adam and Eve at the beginning of Genesis, which is called the Fall, is one such movement. Through disobedience, Adam and Eve forfeit the close relationship with God they enjoyed in the Garden of Eden, and suffer as a result. Many a parent has employed the same interpretive movement when he or she has declared to a child who has come a cropper, 'If you had only done what I asked you in the first place, this would never have happened!' Whenever something goes wrong, the instinct of those with this outlook is to ask who is to blame. A serious difficulty occurs when we put this movement into reverse, and suggest that if someone is suffering, it must be because they were disobedient, and so brought the distress on themselves. (The book of Job is a cry of protest against such an interpretation.)

The southerly outlook

The southerly outlook by contrast has an interpretive movement from chaos or mess or exclusiveness toward harmony and resolution. Arguing with the northerly outlook, a southerner will say it is not so much a matter of disobedience, it is much more likely to be muddle, ignorance or misunderstanding, or even blind obedience to rules and regulations. Peter, according to the New Testament, had to be corrected into a more generous fellowship on at least two occasions when he was tempted to keep the rules and not eat with Gentiles (Acts 10.9–29; Galatians 2.11–14). The book of Proverbs is constantly exhorting us to be wise and avoid foolishness, and it provides plenty of examples of the wisdom it wants to encourage. The emphasis on Jesus Christ as a mediator (as in Hebrews 8.6; 9.15; 12.24, where Jesus is described as the mediator of a new covenant) and reconciler (a Pauline emphasis, especially in Romans 5; 2 Corinthians 5) reflects this movement from distress and alienation toward unity.

The easterly outlook

The easterly outlook, which expects inspiration and adventure, has an interpretive movement from timidity and conventionality toward excitement and empowerment. The world in which we live is frightening and exhilarating at the same time. We are caught up in a battle between good and evil, oppression and liberation, and only with the power of the spirit will we overcome. We find examples of this in Jesus' ministry of casting out evil spirits (demons) and Paul's description of our struggle being 'against cosmic powers, against the authorities and potentates of this dark age, against the superhuman forces of evil in the heavenly realms' (Ephesians 6.12). The metaphors of rescue and escape are used to describe the drama of this particular movement, which occurs in a world of miracle and mystery. The westerly outlook is rejected as being captured by cautiousness and bondage to convention and secularization.

The westerly outlook

The westerly outlook, however, regards itself as practical and pragmatic, seeing its interpretive movement from variability, uncertainty, even wishful thinking, toward reliability and a kind of uniformity. The world is essentially a reliable place in the sense that you can be sure that one event will follow another, as spring and summer follow winter. The blossom will be followed by the fruit, unless frost or disease intervenes, but even these interruptions are reliable in a perverse way. We can understand what happens even when it's unwelcome. Lend – or borrow – too much money and trouble is likely to follow. There's no mystery here; no cosmic powers, just human stupidity, egged on by greed. Jesus asks whether anyone would 'think of building a tower without first sitting down and calculating the cost, to see whether he could afford to finish it' (Luke 14.28). 'The budget' frequently trumps many an attractive vision! We have to be realistic, practical and down to earth. This outlook is not likely to inspire the young or appeal to their idealism, but it points to an inescapable reality. If you build your house on sand it will not survive the first powerful storm (Matthew 7.24–27).

Reconciling opposite outlooks

Reading through these descriptions, you may recognize that each can claim to be a Christian outlook, a fact which has led a number of people in my experience to want to look in all four directions at the same time! This expresses an understandable desire to be comprehensive and all-embracing, but it misses the degree to which each outlook is an implicit rejection at least of the opposite one. In practice it is very difficult for people with opposite outlooks to work well together.

Consider the following pair of statements, the first of which can be seen as representing the northerly outlook and the second the southerly outlook:

People who break the law should be punished severely.
Our priority should be to rehabilitate those who break the law.

These statements are not *logically* incompatible (you might just be able to combine severe punishment with rehabilitation), but they are *practically* incompatible when you recognize that such statements also carry a degree of passion and conviction.

One person sincerely believes that offenders only learn when they are punished harshly; they laugh at you if you are kind to them.

Another sincerely believes that harsh punishments only increase alienation; if we put more time and energy into rehabilitation projects, many offenders would become law-abiding citizens. Each person is convinced that the other is seriously mistaken. Both could, if they were minded to, gather biblical texts and precedents to back up their position, for example, the salutary story of Ananias and Sapphira (Acts 5.1–11) versus that of the woman taken in adultery (John 8.1–11). Each may genuinely respect the other's right to hold his or her opinion, but would they work well together? They would certainly find it very demanding.

Different opinions about what your church needs are even more pertinent to our theme. Let's now consider the following two statements, the first of which represents the easterly outlook and the second the westerly outlook:

> What our church needs is an inspiring vision for the future.
> We need a realistic plan for the development of our church.

One person feels that we need a new vision of what the spirit of God is calling us to be; we must not allow ourselves to become bogged down by timid thinking and business plans based in secular considerations. The other is convinced that we require clear answers to what is in mind, what it will cost, how we will pay for it and who will be responsible for seeing it is all done; we can't allow ourselves to get carried away with unrealistic dreams and ideas which are not rooted in the real world. Each person is convinced that the other is seriously mistaken, and we could imagine a different battle of biblical texts taking place – 'Where there is no vision, the people perish' (Proverbs 29.18, AV; modern translations are not so useful in this particular argument) versus counting the cost (Luke 14.28 again). Would such people work well together?

Logically they might, but practically they will find it very difficult. These differences are not just opinions; they are also policies. And a local church can only follow one policy at a time. This means that one policy will win and the other will lose, at least for the time being. (An alternative is that there will be a stalemate; neither will win and everyone will become frustrated.)

This does not often happen in my experience, because most churches have a shared outlook which naturally dominates. People whose outlook is opposite to the dominant one tend not to feel at home and soon move on. In a few cases, however, the ordained minister has an outlook which is opposite to the congregation's dominant outlook. This can make for considerable unhappiness. Apparently minor misunderstandings or differences (for example, about the minister's non-attendance at a congregational sale of work, or about the right tune for favourite hymns) soon escalate into mutual incomprehension, so that neither party can please the other. These are serious situations and far from easy to resolve.

In such situations only four broad outcomes are possible:

1 The minister moves on.
2 The minister stays and many in the congregation move on.
3 Some kind of understanding and compromise is reached between the minister and the congregation.
4 Everyone blames everyone else and the situation deteriorates further.

I shall try to make some constructive comments about such predicaments in Chapters 8 and 9, but I want here to suggest a way in which the situation might be avoided in the first place, or at least anticipated in a constructive way.

Matching people and congregations

If you have discovered fairly clear and broad agreement in the outlook of your congregation, you may well feel ready to move on to the next chapter. Your dominant outlook will be a factor in the way you do things, and will almost certainly be reflected in the church story, something we will look at in Chapter 6. But if you have discovered that a significant number of people – or a number of significant people – are looking in opposite directions, or if you want to use this test as a way of thinking about what is involved in two congregations working more closely together, or appointing an ordained minister as your leader, it is worth looking rather more carefully at the possible implications.

Sharing exactly the same outlook is probably not healthy for a community. You might be liable to congratulate one another about how wise you are and develop an unconscious complacency, and possibly even feel superior to those who hold other views. But holding opposite outlooks may be even more perilous: you might be liable to serious misunderstandings and conflict arising from the different assumptions about the nature of the world your outlooks imply. People whose outlook is to one side or the other of the dominant outlook can stimulate the congregation by offering a contrasting perspective. If, for example, the dominant outlook were SW (a mix of 'pragmatism' and 'understanding'), a contrasting perspective would be either SE (a mix of 'understanding' and 'vision') or NW (a mix of 'pragmatism' and 'obedience'). This kind of contrast promises the possibility of mutual stimulus, whereas the opposite, NE (a mix of 'obedience' and 'vision'), is likely to produce frustration and mutual incomprehension.

Hopewell at one point calls these different outlooks 'negotiations', which is a very helpful way of regarding them. People – including ourselves – can and do change their minds and their practices, but they need time and room as well as reasons to do so. Learning to negotiate is an important community skill. Several congregations with whom I have shared this way of recognizing our outlook have suggested that there may well be a significant connection between each outlook and age; many of us, when young, value both the certainty of rules and laws and the adventure of dreams and inspiration, but as we grow older we come to be more pragmatic, less idealistic. I think there is a measure of truth in that, certainly for some people, but equally certainly, not for all. For this kind of change, several decades may be needed! If we are

There are other ways of discovering a congregation's outlook

I find this particular framework for helping a congregation begin to recognize its own dominant outlook is simple and works reasonably well, but it is not the only way. Some congregations have been studied with the Myers-Briggs Type Indicator® (as reported, for example, in the *Journal of Adult Theological Education*, 1.1 (June 2004), pp. 65–77). This is a sophisticated indicator of an individual's personality, and requires a qualified practitioner to administer it. The results for a whole congregation suggest important things about how they are likely to learn, what they are likely to be good at and what are their likely weaknesses. Many people have found that the Myers-Briggs Type Indicator® illuminates much about who they are and how they relate to people of a different type from themselves. Building on Myers-Briggs in a different and perhaps more accessible way (because it doesn't require a qualified practitioner), David Runcorn, the author of *Spirituality Workbook: A Guide for Explorers, Pilgrims and Seekers*, offers an imaginative way into discussion and increased self-awareness by suggesting that we invite everyone in a congregation to identify with one of the four living creatures around the throne in Revelation 4, to each of which he gives a 'personality'. The exercise is described in Chapter 9 of his book (pp. 76–83), and would make a good follow-up for people who are either in-trigued by or uncertain about the way I have proposed considering outlooks.

impatient and try to hasten the process of change we may end up making things more difficult.

Summary

The **mirror** simply reveals our dominant outlook. Occasionally this can be surprisingly narrow (all within one quadrant, for example), but more often it is the mean of a distribution that covers about half of the directions. This indicates fairly clearly the kind of things which will resonate with us and the kind of things we might find hard to relate to. For example, a congregation which shares a pragmatic and severely practical outlook is unlikely to respond well to those who urge them to be inspired by a vision for the parish. Equally, a congregation whose outlook involves valuing understanding and education are unlikely to be convinced by an approach which holds that most things can be clarified by reference to a clear verse of Scripture (about divorce, for example, or the ordination of women, or homosexuality).

In the same way, the mirror indicates the kind of people who are likely to be attracted to join us, people with a similar outlook. In God's overall economy there may well be another church in the vicinity to cater for those with an opposite outlook to our own.

As a **health check** the process can help some folk diagnose, in the sense of understand better, why they feel out of place within a particular local church. Their outlook is quite different, which will mean that their instincts, the things they take for granted, the kind of values they appeal to, are all significantly different. At the very least that can be wearing, at its worst it can be intolerable.

Such mutual incomprehension presents very serious problems when the ordained minister is the person (or is among the people) looking in the opposite direction to the majority. Sadly in my experience, this condition is often only diagnosed well after the situation has deteriorated significantly. However, if these questions were asked as part of the appointment process, serious problems might be avoided or at the very least better understood and met in a positive way. Similar observations could be made about two or more congregations being invited (or required) to join or work more closely together. There is more about this in Chapter 9.

The **building design** metaphor perhaps has little to offer, for contrasting outlooks do not of themselves imply contrasting organizational structures.

The metaphor of **practical wisdom** on the other hand will point to the need to recognize the possibility that our outlook may change with time. We will be able to see more of this time-related implication when we look at your church's life cycle in the next chapter. For the moment it would seem natural that a visionary, inspirational outlook belongs more naturally to the 'youth' of a church, and a pragmatic, realistic outlook to the stages of and beyond maturity.

Wisdom may also suggest that the people who are 'on the edge' of the dominant outlook may well have a valuable contribution to make, precisely because they do not see things as the majority do. They may be able to inject some realism into the vision or some adventure into the over-cautious budget.

A significant part of shared wisdom involves learning the skill of negotiation. This is not the art of getting your own way, but the genuine skill of working together to find a good and acceptable way forward. It is a shared skill in the sense that you cannot negotiate alone or with those who refuse to negotiate. Appreciating that other people may well have a different outlook to yours and attempting to put yourselves in their shoes, so to speak, can be important steps on the road to acquiring such wisdom.

★★★

It may seem an impertinent question, but
how do you see the world, Lord?
Or, more exactly,
where should we look for the right kind of development?
We have to confess that we see things
with a mixture of confidence and fear,
well aware that not everyone shares the same outlook as us.

Some of us put our whole confidence in the rules you have given
us,
in Scripture, and the discipline of the church.
If we were really to love you and our neighbour
then everything would be fine and life would be straightforward.
Things go wrong, sometimes dreadfully wrong, when we
disobey,
so we are fearful of going against your laws, even by mistake.
We are convinced that development begins when we go back to
basics,
back to the Bible and obedient faithfulness.

Some of us put our confidence in the guidance of the spirit
who tells us what to do and

inspires us with visions of your will for us.
We wrestle with the spiritual forces of timidity
and the conventionality that follows the herd.
We wrestle too with the dark forces of the spirit world,
claiming victory in the power of your name.
So when things go wrong it is because we have failed to obey the
    vision.
For us development will be an exhilarating adventure
as we listen faithfully to the promptings of your spirit.

Others of us are more afraid of ignorance and stupidity,
which do so much damage to us and to your world.
We put our confidence in education,
in a better understanding of what is happening.
The links between things, cause and effect,
are often hidden and certainly complex:
we need to understand them as we learn
to correct mistakes and discover better ways.
Development for us will mean sorting out the mess and
    confusion
as we learn wholesome ways of going forward.

And some of us feel we should be basically down to earth and
    realistic.
We know enough already to make practical progress,
we should not be dithering about with visions or educational
    programmes,
just get on with the obvious and concentrate on what works.
The kind of development that is going to last will be practical,
and this is usually the result of trial and error,
testing suggestions and going with those that work.

Now we naturally gravitate to one or other of these
    outlooks,
or to a combination of two, but we can't run equally with them
    all
as perhaps you can, Lord.

What are we to do with the outlooks that don't come naturally to
    us?
Should we reject them, undermine them, un-church those who
    hold them dear?
Or is it a matter of mutual acceptance, agreeing to differ?

Or could they prove a useful corrective to the failings inherent in
  our own outlook?
Could our deepest convictions actually contain *temptations*?
Lead us not into temptation – do not bring us to a time of testing –
But deliver us from evil.

5

Stages on a life cycle
Planning for inevitable change

You and I are given this mysterious gift of life only for a while. Our lives have a typical time span, and pass through recognizable stages. We enjoy – I hope – a time as babies and young children; we go to school, pass through adolescence, become young adults and enter what is often called the prime of life. We then move on to maturity (and now the labels become problematic for some), into seniority and old age, and eventually we die. Shakespeare describes how

> one man in his time plays many parts,
> His acts being seven ages.
> *As You Like It*, II.vii.141

Centuries before Shakespeare the writer of Ecclesiastes urged us all to

> Remember your Creator in the days of your youth, before the bad times come . . . (Ecclesiastes 12.1)

And the psalmist, pondering the rapid passing of the years, is moved to pray that we might learn

> so . . . to number our days, that we may apply our hearts unto wisdom.
> (Psalm 90.12; Coverdale's translation in the Book of Common Prayer)

If individuals pass through such stages, do congregations do something similar? And if we can apply our hearts to wisdom as we pass through these stages, can congregations learn to do the same? Although there is some artificiality in the comparison, and a lot of complexity in the detail, I think these are fruitful questions to pursue.

Depicting the life cycle of your church

The simple diagram in Figure 5.1, showing a rising curve levelling off and then declining again, serves as a graphic representation of the life cycle of an individual person (and of many other living things as well). The horizontal axis represents time; the vertical axis is less easily defined but relates to growth and vigour, and also – as we shall see below – has to do with self-sufficiency and dependency.

This diagram can equally well represent the life cycle of a church. Of course it is not representative of everyone or every church, but it does represent typical progress through life for many of us.

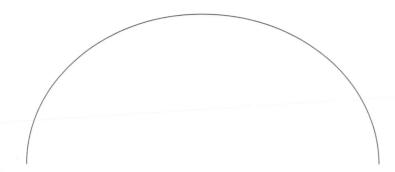

Figure 5.1 A typical life cycle

One of our first challenges is to find appropriate names for the various stages in the life of a church, and to be prepared to face up to some of their typical characteristics. I have set out my own suggestions – influenced by those of others, of course – in Table 5.1 overleaf. It is worth giving careful thought to each stage, but I have found that the last third is usually the most challenging. Two words you may find illuminating in this context are 'aristocracy' and 'bureaucracy'. 'Aristocracy' describes the stage when the church – and its decision making – is dominated by those who have been around longest (the aristocrats). The aristocrats tend to make essentially the same decisions they made the year before, a process usefully labelled 'bureaucracy' because it is like stamping the same old procedures without giving them any serious thought.

Before we explore the implications for a local church in more detail, there are two other features of our life cycle to consider. The first has to do with levels of dependency, the second with the difference between the life cycle of a congregation and that of an individual.

Dependency

Dependency is a basic pattern of life: at the beginning and end of our life most of us find ourselves dependent on others. We can draw a straight line horizontally across the life cycle curve, as in Figure 5.2 (on page 73), to represent the transition from net dependant to net contributor and back to net dependant. As the horizontal line moves up or down, the ratio of net contributors to net dependants alters. We begin life as helpless babies

Table 5.1 Parallel stages in the human life cycle and the life cycle of a church

Human stage	Characteristics	Church stage	Characteristics
Babies	Totally dependent on parents	Brand new	The founders' 'baby'
Young children	Learning to walk and talk with encouragement from parents	Finding our feet	Dependent on the founders for encouragement
Schoolchildren	Learning to read, write and develop skills; dependent on teachers	Learning the traditions	Dependent on teachers for knowledge and knowhow
Adolescents	Learning to become independent, often a stage of rebellion, breaking free of family constraints	Wanting to take responsibility for ourselves	Restlessness over against the influence of the founders/previous generation
Young adults	Finding our way in the wider world, enjoying our independence, sense of adventure, major choices	Exploring possibilities and choosing priorities	Sense of discovery and purpose, increasing confidence
Prime of life	Settling down with major responsibilities (family, job)	Everything up and running	Sense of satisfaction, 'we have arrived'
Maturity	Settled, feel we have learned all we really need to know	Established, a model for others	Complacency creeps in, decisions made by the few (the 'aristocracy')
Seniority	Begin to feel our age, set in our ways, winding down reluctantly	Going stale	Same again, lament the lack of 'others' to do the work we struggle to do
Old age	Increasingly dependent on others (carers, children)	Stagnation	Nothing much happens, closing down or hanging on

completely dependent upon our parents, especially our mothers, for everything we need. We develop an increasing degree of independence as we grow and extend the circle of people upon whom we depend to include teachers, fellow pupils, friends and other communities like clubs and churches. Our dependence on other people never disappears but increasingly we become people who can also contribute to the common good. If all goes well from a conventional viewpoint, we become net contributors to this network of interdependence and stand on our own feet. But unless we meet an early end we eventually find our dependence on other people increasing again, and our capacity to contribute diminishes. We move into a different kind of dependency, requiring help from others according to our particular needs. This may simply be financial help in the form of a pension or other benefit, and, if we live in the UK, free television licences and bus passes. Or it may be to do with mobility or more personal care, like having meals cooked for us, or needing the kind of looking after that a residential home can offer.

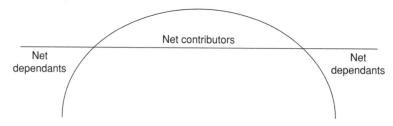

Figure 5.2 **Dependency and the life cycle**

There are several issues to think about as we contemplate dependency.

Valuing dependency

One issue concerns the way we value people who are obviously dependent. At the beginning of life we clearly value their *potential*, so that as a society we regard caring for them – in the widest sense, which includes providing for their education and personal development – as an investment that will be 'repaid' with interest as they move on to become net contributors. At the other end of the life cycle it is more problematic. Many of us (but not all) feel that to become dependent again represents some kind of failure. We hate to think of ourselves becoming a 'burden' to others. We wonder about people whose personalities have died or radically diminished long before their physical bodies die. They represent a challenge and a test for every society, especially one that gives prominence to the value of love, compassion, mutual care and gratitude for what has been given in the past.

Independence and interdependence

Another issue is the way the *balance* between net contributors and net dependants works in a community. At the level of the state this is most easily thought of as an economic problem, which is addressed in different ways by different countries. A common solution is where the net contributors pay – through taxation – for the needs of the net dependants, in addition to providing for their own needs. In times of economic boom this balance is not so difficult to achieve, but in an economic recession it becomes much harder, because the number of dependants increases considerably as contributors lose their jobs. Governments can and do borrow (against future generations' ability to pay) to ease this kind of crisis, but this is not an option open to all. Some draw on reserves (savings) to help them through this kind of crisis, in the hope that in the future they will again be able to make savings and restore the reserves. Many cannot do this and suffer badly as a consequence.

But the balance is not only or even primarily financial. If we do not have enough people qualified and able to make the key contributions that a community needs – as teachers, police officers, bankers and nurses, but also as manufacturers, engineers, designers and retailers (the list is virtually endless) – however much money we have, the society as a whole cannot flourish. The variation in the balance between dependants and contributors can be illustrated in the life cycle figures we have been using by moving the horizontal line up and down. The higher the line, the greater the number of dependants and the fewer net contributors; if the line continues to rise, a point will be reached when the balance is unsustainable.

But what has all this to do with local churches? Compared to the state or many business organizations, the local church is a very small example of an economy, but it is still an important economy which those of us who are concerned about the development of churches need to understand. The viability of churches depends not only on their ability to raise enough money to pay for their activities, but also, and just as crucially, on their ability to utilize the gifts and talents of church members to do the things that are essential and important for Christian churches to do. This relates to the kind of issues we looked at in Chapter 3 when we considered the purposes of the church, and it is a subject we will return to later.

The life cycles of a community

We come to the second important aspect of life cycles. For a family, or for a small community such as a congregation, as opposed to an

Figure 5.3 Overlapping life cycles for families and congregations

individual, life cycles overlap and interact in important ways. Figure 5.3 provides a highly artificial depiction of how the life cycles of different generations interact.

Transferring power

As one generation begins to decline in physical energy and in its ability to make a net contribution, another generation moves from dependency, and its members become net contributors themselves. So the vitality of the family or community does not necessarily increase or decline with the growth and decline of individual members. Within families and communities their shared flourishing depends on the successful transfer of power and responsibility from one generation to the next.

This is frequently a difficult transition for families to make, as can be seen in the example of a family business. The second generation often feels quite prepared to take on full responsibility for running the business long before the first generation is ready to hand that responsibility over. It is not just a question of technological advance (for example, we don't keep on making video cassette recorders now that DVDs are here) but also a matter of prestige and status. If I stand down, what do I stand down to?

Reinventing ourselves

Most successful organizations, so the contemporary wisdom goes, reinvent themselves every few years. In an ideal world they relaunch from the top of the life cycle curve, before any decline is evident. So even as they are successfully doing whatever it is they do, they are at the same time asking, What do we do next? How do we improve our product? What should we stop doing? What should we start doing? If all goes well their life cycle curve will look rather like that in Figure 5.4 (on page 77): growth on top of growth.

It is important to remember that this is an ideal few organizations actually achieve; most small organizations do not survive for very many years, and those larger ones that do frequently do so only by taking drastic steps from time to time: replacing the chief executive at regular intervals, making half the workforce redundant in order to survive through hard times, and such like.

Guidelines for retirement

Many people are very glad to retire from work and embrace the freedom to take up other activities. But equally a good number of people find retirement hard to accept because their own sense of worth and dignity is inextricably bound up with their work and the status it gives them.

The subtle mix of responsibility and honour which goes with many positions in churches can make retirement difficult and forced retirement almost unthinkable. Church office holders can be tempted to hold on to office until they can boast of 20 or 25 years' service (and sometimes a good deal longer than that!). Many people are well aware of the irresponsibility of holding on to office for too long, but nevertheless find it almost impossible to retire. I recall long-standing churchwardens indicating how aware they were of the need to stand down and actually offering to do so, but who were livid when the offer was taken up.

Many churches at denominational level now have clear guidelines, if not rules, about retirement at a specific age or after a certain number of years in post. This represents an organizational wisdom which I think is best followed wherever possible (although occasionally in very small churches it may not be sensible). It has an objectivity which means it is not personal, though I have to admit to meeting some folk who make it personal by simply saying they don't need to take any notice of such things! Such a dog-in-the-manger attitude may help some people feel they are still indispensable, but it does little to build up genuinely healthy local churches.

How can churches reinvent themselves? The most obvious opportunity that local churches have for a relaunch occurs when a new minister is appointed. This can be a complex transition for both minister and congregation, for reasons we will look at more closely in Chapter 8. But for now it serves to illustrate the way the old and new curves meet or intersect, introducing us to another two important elements of the church's life cycle.

In Figures 5.5 and 5.6 I have drawn two possible intersections. The first, as shown in Figure 5.5, is when a new start is made for a congregation in the prime of life, that is to say, one at the top of the life cycle curve. The second, shown in Figure 5.6 (on page 78), is when the congregation is already somewhere 'over the hill' and showing signs of decline.

Figure 5.4 Life cycle curve showing growth upon growth

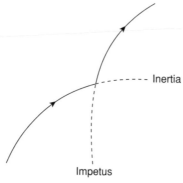

Figure 5.5 Growth from the top of a life cycle curve: 'up and up and up'

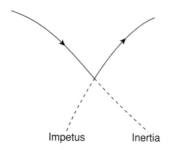

Figure 5.6 Growth after a period of decline: 'down and round and up'

In Figures 5.5 and 5.6 I have drawn a broken line continuing beyond the new start to represent where the congregation was going had the new start not taken place. I have also drawn another broken line coming up from below, as it were, to indicate the new line of development, the impetus for the new start. These broken lines represent important features of change in congregations. A helpful picture comes from ships at sea: a small boat can be turned round comparatively easily; a large vessel, like an ocean-going oil tanker, needs several miles to make a turn once it is under way. Congregations, like sea-going vessels, have a natural inertia. This is not meant as a critical observation, as if inertia were a deplorable thing in a congregation: it is a natural feature of anything that changes or, in terms of the metaphor, that moves.

Inertia and impetus

The inertia of a local church is made up of the habits it has got into and some of the expectations it harbours. Other expectations, and especially hopes and aspirations, contribute to the impetus for a new start. There is an inevitable conflict between this impetus and the church's inertia. Only one of them can dominate, but the other one will always be there to unsettle and disturb, especially at times of transition.

Four stages of growth

Charles Handy observes that most new organizations, and any organization making a new start, passes through four stages. He calls these:

- forming
- storming
- norming
- performing.

We could see these four words as alternative descriptions of the first half of our life cycle for local churches. Forming, self-evidently, describes the initial stages of the life cycle. Storming, many people would agree, is not a bad description of adolescence! In terms of the local church it illustrates the painful decisions and choices that often have to be made whenever the church is developing. Norming is a word invented to fit the sequence, and means establishing the norms or normal patterns of behaviour, procedures, and so on which are an inevitable feature of living and working together. Only when we have done the storming and norming can we effectively perform. Many of us try to avoid the storming; if we succeed, Handy suggests, we will not perform effectively. In the terms I am using, the inertia will apparently have won a decisive victory and continue to dominate.

I do not want to give the impression that I am always on the side of the impetus for change; I am not. Everything depends on the quality of the impetus, balanced against the quality of the inertia. You can have hare-brained or dogmatic impetuses as well as stick-in-the-mud and complacent inertia! The real problem if the storming phase is avoided is that these qualities are not put to the test, and each position avoids the possibility of improving by listening carefully to what the other is saying. This is a major test for the congregation's shared wisdom. Learning how to have a mature, grown-up 'storm' in church life is very important, especially at times of change. Evading the conflict, or conducting it aggressively, as if the other point of view could only be held by idiots, is immature and unwise. Later on we shall be looking more closely at what is involved in making major decisions in local churches; for the moment we will look again at the stages of the life cycle, and notice how they relate to what I have been calling inertia and impetus for development.

Generally speaking, the early, upward-rising part of the life cycle is where we expect to discover aspects of impetus for development. The levelling out and the declining part of the curve is likely to represent inertia. In fact these two forces are nearly always at work together in any local church, and the actual situation is the result of the balance or equilibrium between them. Each can be described as a tradition and can claim to be the proper way to be church. Most churches which are described as mainline or established (not in the technical sense of having a close partnership with the state, but in the ordinary sense of being well established) tend to be dominated by inertia, while the new emergent churches and new expressions of church tend to be dominated by what I have labelled impetus. Notice that I have used a cautious word, 'tend' – it is very unwise to make dogmatic generalizations in this area, for there are always exceptions.

The nature of impetus

Impetus is characterized by excitement, innovation, a sense of discovery and newness, and a tantalizing mixture of confidence and uncertainty – the uncertainty of not knowing what will happen next but expecting it to be good. The impetus tradition emphasizes the newness of the gospel, the 'surprisingness' of God, the adventure of being church. In a paradoxical way this tradition can become established and set in its ways, always concerned with the beginning of the Christian life, looking for conversions and new starts. Its enemy is growing cold, losing that initial love and enthusiasm which first drew us to Christ. Its weakness can be the avoidance of moving on, rather like couples who fear that when the first excitement of falling in love fades, their whole relationship is over. The beginning is just that; wonderful in its way but not the whole story.

The nature of inertia

Inertia is characterized by contentment, being settled, enjoying a familiar routine, and has a different blend of confidence and uncertainty – the uncertainty of fearing that all this might be under threat and may not last for long. The inertia tradition emphasizes the long history of the Church, as if there really was something tangible that 'was everywhere and at all times and by everyone believed', and which must be faithfully maintained. It draws attention to the unchanging nature of God, and to the reliability of the Church in the midst of puzzling change. Its enemy is change for change's sake and a failure to appreciate our rich heritage. Its weakness is the avoidance of moving on, as if we could stay in contented middle age for ever. It wants to hang on to that which only thrives if it is handed on (the basic meaning of tradition).

Managing impetus and inertia

What I want to suggest is that both the impetus and inertia traditions have a role to play in the life of the local church. The tension between them, if understood and managed well, can be a fruitful source of practical wisdom for the congregation. If this tension is not understood and is badly managed, it becomes a source of conflict and unhappiness. The healthy balance between them depends on several things, including where the congregation judges itself to be on the life cycle curve. At an early stage, the rising curve, impetus is clearly and appropriately dominant. As the curve levels out and plateaus, inertia may be appropriately dominant, but as the curve declines again inertia becomes a liability and impetus will be needed to halt the decline. (This is where organizations like local churches and family businesses differ from individuals whose eventual decline and death cannot be avoided.)

Two types of development

Development may happen in quite different ways, depending on where it starts from. Development which begins from near the top of the rising curve increases the steepness of the curve again – it could be described as 'up-and-up-and-up'. Development which begins from a point on the downward curve reverses the trend – it could be described as 'down–and–round–and–up–again'.

The 'up-and-up-and-up' type of development represents an ideal where a church goes on growing and developing. It is constantly innovating and discovering new adaptive ways to be church; it is an exciting and stimulating place to be. It is very appropriate for students and others near the beginning of their adult lives. It will always be a home for the innovators of this world, and in a paradoxical way also for those who see change (usually in the form of repentance and conversion) as the one needful thing.

The difficulty it faces lies in its challenge to the competing inertia; many people will feel that the church has just arrived and they are ready to enjoy it in its mature form. Why should they risk spoiling it all by yet more change? The need for change is not clear, at least not to all. People who have reached the prime of life expect to settle down to a period of stability, even regarding it as a reward for the pioneering work they may have done. They do not want to begin all over again. But what is true for individuals may not be appropriate for organizations, including churches.

In this situation the innovators can seem like upstarts, with the stalwarts saving the church from needless change. Perhaps the innovators want to take out some of the pews to make an open space for people to meet and talk over coffee after the service, while the stalwarts feel such a change would alter the church's traditional layout and that the church hall is a more suitable place for serving refreshments. Some local churches with short time lines (as discussed in Chapter 1), because they have a regular turnover of members (for example, areas dominated by students and young professionals), find the people who might be expected to exhibit inertia have largely moved on to other churches with their developing careers. A long time line might be taken as an indication of stronger inertia.

By contrast, in the 'down-and-round-and-up-again' transition, the innovators are seen as potential saviours and the stalwarts as among those who need rescuing. The difficulty here is with the almost self-contradictory hopes of the majority; we can see the decline and want to reverse it but we also want to keep as much as possible of what we are used to. We would like more people to join us and take up the work, but preferably by continuing the way we do things. We want the younger generation to discover the rich tradition which has nourished us, to appreciate Bach and robed choirs and Merbecke and the old Methodist Hymn Book; we are not so happy when they bring guitars and drums, expect PowerPoint presentations instead of books and take ages to share the peace! It is easy to characterize and apparently trivialize these differences, but they are deep seated and often very difficult to resolve with limited resources.

Large churches can go some way to resolving such tensions by having different services catering specifically for different tastes and age groups. One church I know has five different services each Sunday: an early traditional-language service, a modern communion service with robed choir; all-age worship with a music group; a traditional evening service, again with the choir; and a late evening service for youth with a band and lots of amplification. But few churches have the resources to provide such a range of options, so what often happens is that different churches in an area gain a reputation for, say, traditionalism or modernity, and people travel to the church of their choice. This may be fine for people moving into an area, but it can be very painful if 'your' church changes its style of worship to something you are not used to, or refuses to move toward something you feel is much more up to date. The challenge here is not to say that such changes should not happen, but to discover how to deal maturely with the pain.

The 'down-and-round-and-up-again' transformation will almost always involve facing quite a lot of pain, much of which is difficult to explain. It is not rational, by which I mean that it cannot be eased by argument and discussion alone. Later on we shall look more closely at what is involved in facing the pain of change, but for the moment I merely want to insist that this is a normal and appropriate reaction to change; if we try to ignore it or despise it we only make matters more difficult for the church community as a whole.

Ask everyone what they think

By now you will probably have made your own judgement about where your congregation is located on the life cycle. The first thing I would urge on you is to test your opinion against everyone else's. This is not difficult to do: explain the idea with the help of Table 5.1 (see page 72) and provide everyone with a card or piece of paper with the life cycle curve drawn on it. Then, anonymously, everyone should simply mark the area of the curve where they sense the church is at the moment. When I do this with congregations I usually also ask them to write two or three words to characterize this position – the words are usually taken from the equivalent of Table 5.1.

When the results of all these 'voting papers' are redrawn on to a larger version of the life cycle line, some kind of pattern will emerge. The larger the proportion of members taking part, the more reliable the result of course, but even a dozen people will produce a result that needs to be read carefully. There will be two expressions of opinion: one is the position (or positions) on the life cycle curve, the other is the implication of the words used to describe these positions. I have often been surprised by the results.

Occasionally there will be a high degree of agreement, which can be helpful so far as it goes, but it needs of course to be interpreted. A congregation which locates itself on the rising part of the curve will probably be thinking that it doesn't need much help in developing, since that is already happening. A congregation which locates itself at the top of the curve may be quite happy with its position and reluctant to embrace a transition of the 'up-and-up-and-up' kind. But one which locates itself on the downward part of the curve is revealing that it already senses some kind of decline and is looking for a transition of the 'down-and-round-and-up-again' kind.

Different perspectives on the same 'place'

When I have asked members of a local church to say where they feel their own church is on the life cycle curve, I have usually found a reasonable consensus among the answers, with a majority placing themselves near the top of the downward curve. This makes sense – why would you invite someone who is labelled an Adviser for Parish Development if you were still obviously developing? Sometimes, however, a congregation reveals two clusters on the life cycle curve, usually one on or near the top of the rising curve, the other on or near the top of the declining curve, as shown in Figure 5.7 overleaf.

How do we interpret this kind of answer? There are a number of possibilities:

- One is at first sight paradoxical. The younger generation feels the congregation is 'over the hill', the evidence for this being the large number of older people. But the older generation feels that growth and development is actually taking place, as proved by the presence of the younger generation!
- It may not be so much a generational matter as a difference between an upbeat leadership who insist that all is thriving and a more realistic, or at least unconvinced, congregation who sense that the leadership is whistling in the dark.
- Or it may just be a contrast between newcomers who sense a freshness and vitality (in contrast perhaps to where they have come from) and stalwarts who sense that 'things aren't what they used to be'.

However we read it, two things are important:

1 A tension has been revealed and needs to be addressed.
2 Each 'cluster' (you may well not have thought of yourselves as being in a kind of cluster, but I need a neutral label for the moment!) needs to appreciate and listen to the other if this tension is to be fruitful rather than destructive.

The tension can be described as being between two different perceptions of the same situation. Since congregations are complex entities, both perceptions will have a degree of validity, but it is very important to hold back from saying that one is right and the other wrong. A congregation is made up of different people at different stages with different needs who are all trying to worship and serve God as revealed in Jesus Christ. We ought to expect these different perceptions and seek to live with them in a constructive way. They could be seen as a sign of the tension between impetus and inertia, a tension with real potential for a fruitful outcome.

How this might happen will become clearer if we simply redraw the two-cluster diagram (Figure 5.7) so that the clusters coincide but the curves collide – see Figure 5.8.

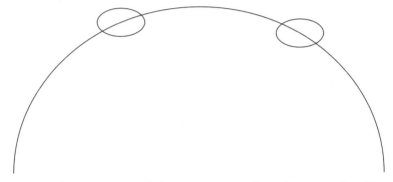

Figure 5.7 Two views of the congregation's position on the life cycle

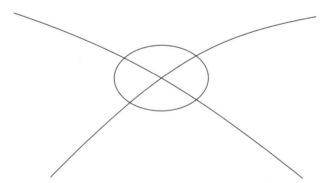

Figure 5.8 Redrawing of Figure 5.7 to reveal where the congregation might be

We now have something that reminds us of the generational transitions we drew in Figure 5.3 (on page 75); the rising curve cluster represents an impetus for change, the declining curve cluster represents the inertia, and any change will be of the 'down-and-round-and-up-again' kind.

What will be involved if each cluster is to appreciate and listen to the other?

- One possibility is that the dominant group (probably the leadership, though the leadership may itself be divided) may have to recognize that its view – located in one of the clusters – is not the only view. It can often happen that a congregation is very reluctant to say hard things to dominant people, who have probably given years of devoted service and gained a rightful place in people's affections, and yet are now in danger of blocking progress. (It's like having to tell Grandad he ought to stop driving.) This anonymous voting may have revealed an important disagreement which cannot easily be put into direct words because to do so would be unacceptably harsh. But revealed in this indirect way, it becomes a test of the leadership's maturity and humility if they can receive it as something other than rejection. (And if the leadership becomes aware that others feel it has been whistling in the dark – it will almost certainly know that already – the result- ant confession will be mutually liberating!) The maturity of the other cluster will consist in giving them room and freedom to hear what is being said.

- Another possibility is to negotiate an agreement to work together at finding a way forward. This may sound so preliminary as to be hardly worth mentioning, but it is not. *Sharing* the responsibility for development is quite different from one group seizing it from the other or one group abdicating to the other. Quite what is involved in working this out will be the major theme of Part 2 of this book.

Summary

Looking in the **mirror** gives us a picture of where we might be as a congregation in terms of growth, stability or decline. (All the words we could use have their drawbacks; here I simply mean to describe three equal segments of the life cycle curve.) This reflection shares the advantage with all the exercises in this book of having been produced by the people themselves. It belongs to them and they are likely to take it seriously. In particular, it provides an initial indication of what devel- opment in general might mean:

- development during the growth stage will seem like 'more of the same', a light touch on the rudder, not especially radical;
- development during the stability stage is likely to be felt as change for change's sake, not really necessary;
- development during the declining stage will be seen as essential and urgent, though the nature of what needs to change may still be a matter of dispute.

In this way the mirror helps us recognize the nature of development in our particular circumstances. It may also be a way of telling the leadership – or any other group who may be surprised by the reflection in the mirror – something they are reluctant to recognize. The interpretation of the significance of what the mirror reveals is also part of the congregation's task and responsibility.

The **health check** may indicate the likely symptoms of poor health to look out for at each stage:

- The hazards of growth are those of youthful enthusiasm, overconfidence leading to overcommitment (to an ambitious building project, for example), or to bitter disputes and rivalries.
- The hazards of stability are quite different: self-satisfaction, complacency and an assumption that this stage could last indefinitely.
- The hazards of decline are on the one hand panic and fear, looking for quick cures (the kind of thing Studdert Kennedy, better known as 'Woodbine Willie', called 'Gawdsakery' – 'for Gawd's sake do something!'), and on the other, apathy and depression, a feeling that little can be done to improve the situation.

A different 'symptom' is likely to be a feeling of tension between generations. There is a shared responsibility to make this a fruitful tension, leading whenever possible to wholesome development. This will be easier to achieve when the tension is recognized as a natural and healthy feature of any congregation at certain stages in its life. The reflections and exercises suggested in this chapter may help everyone involved to recognize such tension as a shared predicament, which they have discovered together. The ideal solution is to negotiate a positive outcome for both generations, rather than a victory for one generation and defeat for the other, which would involve a weakening of the whole body.

The arrival of a new minister is an important opportunity for development (it will always be an occasion for change, even when the minister sets out to keep things as they are). Such an opportunity will involve increased tension: people will feel uncertain about what might happen. This is a quite natural response and not a symptom of trouble.

The **building design** metaphor points us toward an approach which expects and enables development as a regular part of life, much as buildings need regular maintenance and repair. For local churches this will generally involve the handing on of responsibility and power from one generation to the next. Some churches, especially at denominational level, have introduced retirement ages for clergy and some lay officers, as well as time restrictions (for example, a maximum of six consecutive years) for certain office holders. This represents a 'constitutional' awareness of the need to encourage retirement on objective criteria rather than having to resort to ousting a long-serving member. This can be helpful, but it is not always appropriate, especially for small churches with few people, and in many cases even where it might be desirable, it is simply ignored.

The **practical wisdom** needed to recognize and allow for these aspects of congregational life which the life cycle has drawn to our attention has at least two main features. One is the wisdom needed to manage different kinds of change; another is the general management of tradition in the sense of handing on responsibility rather than allowing – or sometimes requiring – people to hold on to power and responsibility at the expense of wholesome development.

Both these aspects will be discussed further in Part 2; for the moment it is perhaps enough to observe that when these issues are brought to the attention of as many members of a congregation as possible simply by asking the questions raised in this chapter, there is a better basis for a shared understanding of what is involved than if we simply resort to saying 'These are the church's rules about retirement.' There is a wisdom built into the way we learn things!

★★★

We can't help being as old as we are, Lord!
Age is not just in the eye of the beholder.
Each of us has a real date of birth;
each of us will have a real date of death as well.
And there are advantages, as well as drawbacks, to most ages too.

It can be a real privilege to be a youngster,
flourishing within a community which knows and delights in
  you
(though the church can sometimes have ambitions and standards
which you know even at this early stage are not ones you can
  honestly share).

There is a bitter sweetness as you struggle for your own
  identity,
through the years of formal education with
that mix of rebellion and conformity which tends to satisfy no
  one
as you pass through it.
But then you emerge as your own person
with keys and a PIN to prove it.

You begin to make your way in the world
with a job or a career,
perhaps a partner with whom you can share the intimacies of life,
and a role to play in the life of the church.
It can be very exciting and fulfilling
but it can be a fragile time too.
There can be too much to do,
too many things to hold in balance.
Your career, your partner and your church all ask for more,
but there is only so much that you can give.

Having weathered the storms of early adulthood you can settle
down
into the comfort and safety of modest achievements;
a home, a good job, family and church responsibilities,
adding up to a valuable reputation.
But is that all there is? Shouldn't there be more to life than this?
Is the drawback a strange emptiness at the heart of all this apparent
success?
You find a new role or a new way of understanding who you
are,
a way of emerging from the cramping chrysalis of a mid-life
crisis
into the relative freedom of maturity and inner peace.

You can enjoy life without having to prove yourself,
you can receive without feeling guilty,
you can do your own thing and be your own person,
at home, at work and in church.

Then it gradually becomes clearer that even this stage comes to a
close.
Retirement is a challenge; who are you now the job is over?
You look back on success and failure, with thankfulness and
regret.
You seem to have more time, but this is only partly true,
or at least only true for a while as the energy declines
and the routine tasks take longer and longer.
You can't be as independent as you want to be
as you surrender to the help and care of others.

And how do we live together through all these stages?
Is one 'ideal' and the rest simply preparation and sequel?

Should one stage dominate and the rest play only a supporting
  role?
How do we who can only be at one stage at a time
give to and receive from those at different stages?

May our love keep on growing more and more,
together with true knowledge and perfect judgement,
so that we will be able to choose what is best.

6

The importance of home
Reasons for choosing a local church

One intriguing question I suggest we ask ourselves – and one another – in a congregation is quite how and why we came to be members of our particular church. For some the simple answer is that this is where we have always been: we were born into it. For others it may be the result of a conscious search: we visited several churches in the area before deciding this one suited us best. For a few it may be in response to a clear call from God: 'This is where I want you to be.'

However difficult or easy we find it to answer such a question, it is one which is worth pursuing. If we describe our membership of a particular church as involving a choice, it is certainly the complicated kind of choosing which is more than the rational weighing up of advantages and disadvantages. It is a process that involves a range of factors, including a strong element of feeling at home, being comfortable enough to stay.

James Hopewell in his book *Congregations* helps us explore the subject by suggesting that choosing a local church is rather like searching for a home, a house to live in. When we look for a place to live, he suggests, there are four main factors that determine our choice. These are:

1 contextual
2 mechanical
3 organic
4 symbolic.

Each plays a part, but one of the four generally dominates.

The contextual factor is described by estate agents in the UK as location, and is often felt by them to be the most decisive factor. We choose somewhere to live because of its location – it is in the catchment area of good schools, it has good communications, it's convenient for shopping and recreation and so on. There will be locations that are convenient but are felt to be poor for one reason or another and others that are unsuitable because they are too expensive. We choose a context that is both convenient and in which we can feel at home, which usually means the sort of neighbourhood we are used to. Some people couldn't live in the centre of a large city; others would judge a rural location out of the question.

The mechanical factor has to do with the state of the building and how well it does its job. Does the survey report any significant defects? Have there been problems with drains or the heating system? How expensive will it be to run and maintain? These sorts of questions highlight the condition of the potential home and its practicality for us. The location may be just right but if the house needs too much doing to it, or promises to be very expensive to run, then it's not for us.

The organic factor points to the scope the house offers for us to do the things we want to do at home. Is it large enough for all the family? Or is it too big now we are approaching retirement? Will the garden be too small or more than we can cope with? These are more than merely mechanical issues. If, for example, the family includes members who work from home or who need a quiet place to do their homework, then a house that lacks enough space may generate tensions and frustrations which damage family life.

The symbolic factor is more difficult to define. I have often called it the 'feel' of a house (a word Hopewell does not use). It is that factor which tells you almost instantly that one house will not do, but another is just right. They may both be satisfactory from the point of view of the first three factors, but one is 'us' and the other isn't. The house we choose to live in says something about us; it projects an image of who we are, or would like to think we are. Different people inevitably read images in different ways – a house that is too grand, too posh for one family may be just right for another family who don't regard it as posh or grand at all.

The four factors and the study of congregations

Hopewell relates these four factors to different ways in which congregations can be studied.

Contextual

A contextual study focuses on the place of the local church in the wider world. In very general terms it has been associated with the idea that the world should set the agenda for the church; in other words the mission of a local church depends very much on the needs and circumstances of the local community. Such observations point to important contrasts, for example, between rural and urban mission, and within these broad distinctions to the differences between a rural community in the mainly arable farmland of East Anglia and the hill farms of Cumbria; or between an urban parish in a large seaside town and one in the inner city areas of Manchester or Birmingham. The location to a large extent shapes the mission, though it is possible for a local church to ignore its immediate context and be almost entirely inward looking.

Mechanical

A mechanical study of churches looks at how the church functions; does it use its resources and opportunities effectively? Such a study is likely to focus on the church's annual report, including the statistics of attendance, the level of giving and the number of projects undertaken. The health of the church will be judged by figures like these. Hopewell suggests that church growth principles, popular especially in the 1970s in studies of growing churches carried out by writers such as Donald MacGavran and Peter Wagner, basically reflect this mechanical perspective. Wagner, for example, emphasizes 'seven vital signs' of a healthy church, which include dynamic leadership, a mobilized laity, homogenous membership, proven evangelistic methods, and biblical priorities. The implication seems to be that if these principles are followed, growth will automatically follow.

Organic

An organic study of congregations, by contrast, rejects as far as it can the mechanical metaphor in preference for seeing the local church as an organism, a living entity with a life and character of its own. Is this life healthy and wholesome or is it dysfunctional? How do people relate to one another? Are members real participants or are they just spectators? Is this place a fellowship, in which we can grow in faith, in which our children will be nurtured and which challenges us about the quality of our Christian discipleship? These may loosely be described as 'quality' questions, in contrast to the 'quantity' questions which characterize the mechanical approach.

Another way of looking at this aspect of a congregation is to think of the scope for personal involvement the local church offers. This is not a simple thing to describe because the scope one person is looking for may be quite different from another's. A highly simplified test might be whether you feel a local church is glad to welcome you and discover what role you might play according to your own gifts and needs, or whether it wants you to fit into a predetermined category of its own.

Symbolic

The symbolic study of a congregation seeks to understand the meaning which a church offers to its members. The same church may convey quite contrasting meanings for different members and indeed for non-members too. I recall being surprised when someone told me that a particular church in the locality (not the one I belonged to) was for 'the snobs' and for this reason, she wouldn't go there. Some people are suspected of attending certain churches because of the kudos or status it gives them; others rejoice in being part of a humble set-up and avoid any hint of 'prestige' (though they might want to insist that theirs is the kind of church 'where the real work gets done'). Many people don't consciously think in these terms at all, though this doesn't mean that they are not influenced in important ways by such matters. Put at its simplest, there are certain churches in which you feel at home and others where you don't. You may not be able to explain what makes the difference, but you nevertheless 'feel' it!

Asking the congregation

This would be a good point at which to investigate the role these four different factors play in the life of your own local church. Any further reflections will then be in dialogue with a real situation rather than with my account of a supposedly typical church or your own guesswork.

When the four reasons have been explained and illustrated, you could offer everyone a simple voting slip, asking them to distribute ten votes between the four factors so as to reflect their own position, just as was suggested when examining the four purposes of the church in Chapter 3. The votes are then counted and a percentage share for each choice calculated, which can be represented again as a pie chart. Alternatively there is a simpler and quicker method: invite people to regard the room they are in as being divided into four quadrants, each representing one of the four factors. Everyone simply moves to stand in the quadrant (or on the boundary between quadrants) which best represents their reason for choosing this church. You can count and record the numbers standing in each quadrant, but you already have an instant impression of how people have voted.

Whenever I have done this with a congregation there has nearly always been some support for each option, but far and away the most votes have been given to the symbolic, the 'feel' of the congregation. What might our result mean?

Achieving a balance

The first observation I would offer concerns the important contribution that *each* approach makes. Symbolic may be decisive for most, but you cannot ignore the context, the mechanics or the organic nature of local churches. It is important to keep a balance. It is easy for me to write this from the vantage point of my desk, much more difficult to achieve in the life of real local churches.

The result of taking a vote in this way should provide some helpful clues. It may be that the option which received the smallest number of votes points to a potential or actual weakness. For example, if the mechanical approach receives little or no support – on the grounds that you are certainly not a machine and that quality is much more important than quantity – you still cannot thrive if you ignore completely issues to do with the budget and other matters connected with the viability of the church. If context came last, are you in danger of neglecting the needs of the local community in which God has placed you? In this way, ask yourselves whether the option with the lowest number of votes might not already be a weakness needing attention.

You can also use this result to interpret your own history, the local church story we looked at in Chapter 1. For example, a good number of churches have in recent years added kitchens and toilets to the facilities available in their church building. This has been a welcome improvement in most cases, but it hasn't often made a hoped-for difference to the continuing life of the church. Occasionally we have invested an 'organic' hope in a 'mechanical' improvement, and then been disappointed that what we hoped for didn't happen.

It is helpful to recognize that different people, and especially different church bodies, will look at local churches from different standpoints, which Hopewell's four factors can help us appreciate. For example, central church bodies (like dioceses) which ask for financial contributions and collect statistics are largely dominated for these purposes by the mechanistic view. Without the money and the statistics which enable them to calculate a fair contribution from each local church, they cannot do their job of supporting all the local churches and especially the ordained ministers (including a range of 'hidden' tasks like providing pensions, housing for clergy, legal services and the like). Broadly speaking the accounts department of almost any organization can be successfully run along mechanistic lines, and this feature of an organization's life might be regarded as an aspect of the constantly moving and changing foundation which enables all the other things to happen. The fact that it is not at the top of our agenda does not diminish its significance.

Strategic planning

Another clue this exercise might give us concerns strategic planning. I think it is likely that the dominant reason we have for choosing a particular church will also be a dominant reason for those who might join us. In other words, the strategic priority will be to focus especially on that aspect of our church life. At the very least we could think imaginatively about what each perspective might suggest.

Contextual

The context or location is something to celebrate. You may be able to strengthen your links with community events which are already happening, like an annual gala or village fete or Our Parish in Bloom. Or you could promote an exhibition of your church's story (as suggested in Chapter 1) and invite other groups to join with their own exhibitions; for example, the local scouts and guides could be asked to contribute a display about their history. You could organize a Fun and Games afternoon for all ages, or sponsor a community litter pick. Or, if it is appropriate for your context, you could arrange for exchange visits to local mosques, synagogues, temples and the churches of other denominations. Occasionally the context may confront us with something challenging and controversial, like the rise of fascist groups or the sudden influx of asylum seekers, or the need to make the church building available for people looking for a way to respond to a major trauma in the life of the community.

Mechanical

The mechanical aspect needs regular review in most churches. This frequently takes the form of an inspection of the building or a stewardship renewal campaign or a major fundraising project. These are specialized areas for which numerous published resources are available; therefore I shall not elaborate on them here.

Organic

The organic aspect of church life is perhaps more difficult to review. It is evident both in the things we do together as a church and in the informal relationships which are involved within and around these more obvious events. One of the unconsciously limiting features of the way many churches function is that there are few occasions for a general shared reflection on what is happening and the value of what we are busy doing. We have a lot of services of worship and meetings of a formal or structured kind (I'm thinking of all the subgroups that are frequently an important part of the life of churches – women's groups, Mothers' Union, men's societies and the like, as well as the activities for youth and children), as well as formal decision-making meetings, like church boards or church councils.

It would be helpful for this organic aspect of our life together to hold open meetings from time to time at which we could review matters like how we care for the housebound, how we welcome newcomers and visitors, how we involve children and adults with special needs, how we frame our prayers of intercession, the place of music in our worship and so on. There are a surprising number of worthwhile topics, especially if we include aspects of our activities that we may not otherwise reflect on, like the possibility that we are being racist in some of the things we do, or that we go out of our way to avoid even talking about issues like homosexuality. These 'open meetings' are not to be thought of as places to criticize people and practices, still less to issue instructions or lay down policies in any formal way (for example, by passing resolutions), but as occasions when our shared responsibility for the quality of what we do and are is recognized and reviewed, and where people have an opportunity to make constructive suggestions. The method of large group consultation known as Open Space Technology is especially suitable for this. (Some information about how Open Space Technology works can be found in Chapter 9.)

Symbolic

The symbolic is probably even harder to review, mainly because it is made up of aspects of ourselves as individuals and as communities which we do not often address directly and which in any case are not always accessible to rational analysis or discussion. What follows, therefore, is a more detailed consideration of how we might strategically approach symbolic elements in our local church.

The symbolic perspective

The symbolic is a powerful vehicle for deeply rooted traditions. So, for example, in communities where in the past those who worked for the dominant employer were required to attend church more or less as a condition of their employment, staying away from church may now be an important symbol of their freedom from this kind of constraint. Such ideas often reside relatively far back in people's memories but are passed on from one generation to the next in the form of what outsiders will be tempted to describe as prejudice.

Yet symbols mean different things to different people. Paradoxically it could now be a symbol of freedom from the prejudices of the family for someone to join a church, and demonstrate his or her personal liberation from the constraints of family convictions and customs. But rebellion against the family is very different from a symbolic defiance of an employer.

Clashes over the symbolic may come to a head in what are often called 'mixed marriages', especially when one or both parties have given up the religious traditions of their parents and grandparents. Although such traditions may seem to have lost their place in the lives of the people concerned, their residual power makes itself evident when those people are invited to accept a different tradition instead. If you have for all practical purposes ceased to be an Anglican or Presbyterian or Catholic or Jew or Muslim and want to marry someone who has also given up practising but from a different background, the powerful symbolism of where you marry and what form the marriage ceremony takes can nevertheless generate intense conflict. It is often impossible to satisfy either tradition, and some compromises have to be made, but even then some traditions can be very dismissive of other traditions, saying, for example, that the couple are not properly married, or even going as far as disinheriting them.

The symbolic and the church's reputation

What applies to individuals applies in a different way to congregations and local churches. The symbolism does not lie, wholly or even mainly, in obvious symbols like incense, candles and elaborate or simple rituals, or even in the church building itself; much of it is carried by the church's story and reputation. A church that has an ancient building and which has been at the heart of the local community for centuries tends, rightly or wrongly, to regard itself as an essential part of that community, and to be entitled to turn to it for help when, for example, the roof needs major repair. If the wider community also assumes the church is essential then that help is usually forthcoming. It is often surprising and encouraging for churches of this kind to discover just how much the wider community values a church building it hardly ever attends.

But a new church in a new community does not enjoy that kind of support; it has to gain a reputation for something the community recognizes as worthwhile, like providing support for families during the miners' strike or working tirelessly with the youngsters on the estate, before it will gain much support from those who do not come. By the same token, a reputation for being aloof – 'they wouldn't baptize our Tracy' – however undeserved, will work against the support of the wider community.

Local churches are often not very aware of their reputation in the neighbourhood, and when they are, frequently think to themselves that many criticisms which are made are quite unjustified and so can be ignored. While it is important not to be neurotic about our reputation, it is important to pay attention to it and if possible to correct serious misrepresentations. The reputation of a church has a symbolic impact on those who might join: 'They are only after your money', 'It's nearly all elderly people', 'It's a happy-clappy place', 'They focus mainly on the children.'

Some churches, at least in the UK, have long been associated with a particular class, so that if you belonged to a different class attending might be seen as 'getting above yourself' or 'pretending to be something you're not'. These are subtle but powerful barriers for many people and they are not confined to churches. Are there certain shops we would not enter because they are either too posh or too cheap? Would we still travel by taxi even though a bus would get us to our destination on time? Are there newspapers we would never buy? Many things are chosen or rejected not on intrinsic merit but because of what they say about us.

The symbolic and the church's story

The church's story itself is symbolic, as we began to see in Chapter 1. Some churches I know have met major problems and overcome them; in one case, the roof was badly damaged in a storm and it was 18 months before the repairs were complete. But in that time the congregation met in the church hall, much less formally, got to know each other much better and came to regard the calamity with the roof as a blessing in disguise. Their story is one of overcoming adversity.

Another church has suffered a number of serious setbacks and has become despondent; its members feel let down by God, clergy and the powers-that-be and seem to be waiting for a knight on a white charger to come riding to their rescue. They feel badly treated, and complain that other people just don't recognize how difficult their situation is.

Another church again experienced a golden age in the recent past when the church was full of new life; if you came late you wouldn't get a seat and everything was wonderful. But it all went downhill after the original minister moved on and they have been struggling ever since. They haven't been able to find a minister capable of doing what he did.

The symbolic nature of these stories does not reside in their truth, in the sense of their accuracy as accounts of what has happened. It has more to do with what many people describe as resonance. If my own personal or family history includes the overcoming of adversity and the finding of unexpected blessings through apparent disasters, I am likely to resonate with the first church's story; if I feel badly let down by everyone else or I'm trying to recapture a time when I was obviously very successful, then the other two stories will resonate more with me.

The story carries a meaning and this is usually clear in the way the story is told. But the meaning is not necessarily an inseparable part of the story, by which I mean that it is possible to interpret the facts of the story in more than one way. Recognizing that we have a choice in the way we tell our stories – without altering the events but seeing them in a different light – is both a sign of maturity, and part of what it means to develop in a positive way.

> ### Differing interpretations in the Bible
>
> One of the clearest biblical demonstrations of how a story can have a choice of possible meanings is the interpretation which Joseph places on his brothers' attempt to harm him, recorded in Genesis 45: 'Now do not be distressed or blame yourselves for selling me into slavery here; it was to save lives that God sent me ahead of you' (v. 5). We could imagine the possibility that Joseph might have been so damaged by his brothers' actions that he spent the rest of his days bewailing his misfortune. If he did pray that God would rescue him – which is, I think, what most of us would have done in the circumstances – the prayer was not answered in the most obvious and straightforward way. Instead Joseph was able in due course to see the pattern of his life opening up possibilities for good which might not have happened any other way. It is an example of St Paul's audacious claim that 'We know that all things work together for good for those who love God' (Romans 8.28, NRSV Anglicized).

The symbolic has also to do with the sense of whether we feel at home in a particular church or whether we feel ourselves welcome as guests, tolerated as newcomers or resented as interlopers. These are things most people feel instinctively rather than learn from any words that may be spoken; or rather, we sense such things from the tone of the words and not from their literal meaning. It is possible to say 'Come on in! You are welcome' with genuine enthusiasm, with reluctance, or with heavy sarcasm. Most of us pick up this sort of thing very quickly, and equally give out such messages almost without thinking. It happens when people move into a village, a street, a block of flats, or visit a restaurant or café, as well as when they come through the doors of a church.

One particular church became increasingly conscious of its declining numbers and aware that it didn't have enough people to do all the things they were used to doing, so the congregation began to pray for people to come along. After a few months they felt seriously frustrated – no one had joined them! Then they looked more closely at what was happening. There were actually about three newcomers a month; but to their horror they realized that these were not the kind of people they were praying for. These were wounded people, damaged people, people who would take up quite a lot of their time and energy if they were to welcome them wholeheartedly into the fellowship. God, they felt, was sending them the wrong kind of people.

This chapter has been about something elusive but significant: the experience of feeling at home, finding our comfort zone, as some would say. Most Christians will probably sense that we face a paradox here – it is important not to stay entrenched in the comfort of our homes, for God is calling us to do new things, to break down these invisible barriers and discover a larger and more generous fellowship; and yet we need a home, we need to know who we are and where we really belong if we are not to be totally at sea in this wider world. The New Testament suggests a piece of practical theology for negotiating with this paradox, which is to practise hospitality and welcome strangers. This leads to the possibility of entertaining angels unawares, a possibility many of us never contemplate!

Summary

Looking in this particular **mirror** will have reflected back to us some of the factors which influence our choice of a church and the values we are looking for. Typical results suggest that the more rational criteria like location, condition and scope – matters that you can argue about – are not as significant as the less obviously rational (in the sense that you cannot easily argue about it) factor of the symbolic, the feel of the church. Most local churches turn out to be for 'people like us'.

This may help us recognize two important things:

- While Christ is for all kinds of people without exception, local churches in practice are not (a reason for humility and ecumenism).
- The reason why most of us choose a particular church is not confined to rational considerations. This serves as a reminder of the essential mystery at the heart of both individuals and communities.

The **health check** relates to the physical and environmental factors that contribute to our health or illness. Just as poor living conditions may lead to poor health, unhappiness with our surroundings can make us ill, leading us perhaps to ask, Am I living in the right house? This is a difficult question for individuals to ask themselves but nevertheless important.

Finding a church in which you feel at home and in which you can flourish is important for an individual's health. But there are other important considerations to bear in mind, such as loyalty and commitment to others. In the same way, re-roofing the church building may be a necessity if we are to keep it in good repair, but no one expects it will revitalize our mission!

The **building design** metaphor may help us recognize in these househunting reflections the very subtle complexity of what church means for many people. It presents us with some insight into the dimensions of very difficult choices: for example, how an old and inconvenient building can be treasured above somewhere much better able to accommodate all we want to be as a church, yet lacking the history.

In terms of our **practical wisdom** we find ourselves approaching more closely to that vital facility of judgement, the capacity to achieve a fruitful balance between these different aspects of church life. What I want to encourage is the perception that this wisdom is something that is shared and that every member can contribute to it. This is a theme that will be addressed directly in Part 2.

***

We could adapt Joshua's challenge
Choose you this day whom you will serve
and ask why did we choose this church and not another?
Perhaps it was chosen for us, the church we grew up in.
Maybe because it was nearest or
because it had great facilities or
because it offered all we wanted for the children or
just because it felt right somehow, in a way hard to define.

Maybe we don't really know, maybe it was a mix of all these.
Does it matter, Lord?
All churches are going to have a mix of advantages and drawbacks,
Things they do very well and things they miss completely,
So we choose a package deal, as it were.
You can't pick and mix to select an ideal church,
all advantages and no drawbacks.

But church does also reflect back on us in important ways,
It says something about who we are.
This is encouraging and disturbing at the same time.
Respectability, uprightness and trustworthiness are
valuable reputations for people and for churches
but then the Pharisees probably had all these
and Jesus wasn't too happy with them.

What are we really offering, Lord?
Is it good news for everyone, or mainly for the likes of us?
Why did we choose this church?
It looked like an innocent question
but it raises all kinds of issues – including developmental issues.
What do we really want to develop?
and for whose sake?

7

Our context limits us and gives us scope

Some other important factors which make us unique

By now we have collected, or at the very least thought about, six important characteristics that contribute to who we are as a local church. There are more, of course, but if we just keep on adding to them, our considerations will become very difficult to manage. I think these six characteristics provide a very useful starting point for reflecting on what appropriate development might mean for us. But before we turn to address that question more directly, it is important to mention some other basic factors we are likely to take for granted, just because they are so familiar to us. These too contribute to the uniqueness of who we are and the appropriateness, or otherwise, of our following certain kinds of development. They can all be related to our particular situation, understood in its broadest sense, and can be summarized as follows:

- our geographical and social context
- our cultural and intellectual context
- our moral and ethical context.

Let us now consider in turn each of these contexts, and how it is changing.

Describing our own context

Rather than trying to find the descriptions that geographers or sociologists might use to define your context, here is a simple exercise which can help you collect your own views and impressions. Simply work in small groups on a series of questions like these:

- How would you describe our area?
- What are its main features?
- What attracts people to come and live here?
- What keeps people here?
- What attracts or forces people to move away from here?
- What are the best things about our area?

- What are the worst things about living here?
- How do most people earn a living? (The answer will be a list)
- How do you think people from our neighbouring communities see us?

The responses can then be put together and displayed, or copied into a printed report. Once a group of people start discussing questions like these, other issues arise as a richer picture is built up, reflecting the complexity of the area and the ways in which it is changing.

The geographical and social context

The geographical and social context of a local church may at first sight seem easy to describe, but it rapidly becomes more challenging when you look carefully. It is rare, for example, for people to agree about whether or not an area is affluent. This is due partly to our varying standards for judging affluence, and partly because many people live very close to the upper limit of what they can afford and so always feel comparatively poor. Quite a lot of both wealth and poverty is hidden, sometimes in strange ways even from those experiencing it themselves. So I have come across apparently very wealthy people who, it turns out, were living way above their means, and poor folk eking out a frugal existence despite tens of thousands of pounds in the bank! (You learn this sort of thing when you regularly take funerals.)

Your group discussions will have revealed an impression or set of impressions of your neighbourhood which can be placed alongside your church's story (which we looked at in Chapter 1). They may illuminate each other; take the example we have looked at before, of a congregation with a short time line (whose members have belonged for 25 years or less). This church may turn out to be placed in an area with a rapid turnover of population due to the proximity of training facilities (hospitals, universities) which attract young professionals for a while before they move on to establish careers somewhere else.

Or a village church may recognize that a recently built housing estate has attracted a large number of people who simply want their home to be a dormitory and whose social and economic, and sometimes church life is focused in the nearby city from which they came. Are they commuting from home to work and what they see as 'life', or is it the other way round? Such newcomers contrast strongly with the families who have lived in the village for several generations, and who see it as the natural centre of their world. The newcomers see attractive modern housing with a wonderful view over the fields, while the long-established villagers lament the loss of the hedges where the chaffinches nested, and the old paddock where horses used to be kept as far back as great-grandfather could remember. The church is a 'visual amenity' for the newcomers, not the focus of memories of weddings and baptisms and funerals that it provides for the 'real' villagers. So a contrast, a tension is revealed which presents a challenge to the local church.

The cultural and intellectual context

One thing the above description of the new housing in the village brings to light is that for many people it has resulted in a change in their cultural context. One way of expressing this is by contrasting mobile and settled people. As soon as we do this we need to recognize that this has been a regular and recurring contrast over many generations. Certainly the Bible reveals quite a lot of tension between the purity of the nomadic life and the potential decadence of settled life in cities – in Genesis 11 it is not just the tower of Babel but also the city itself which shows how human beings are in danger of proving that nothing is beyond their reach. This is not a simple matter though; the New Testament is rather more sympathetic to cities, seeing the heavenly Jerusalem as our ultimate home.

Mobile and settled communities

The two patterns of life – mobile and settled – tend to display different cultural characteristics.

The settlers know their locality and all the key people. Their patterns of buying and selling are not just commercial transactions, they are social relationships as well; we stay loyal to people who have treated us well, we avoid those who have cheated us in the past. We know who we can trust and who to keep at arm's length. We appreciate the implicit hierarchy of authority and dignity which is involved in the network of relationships. We will never publicly disagree with old Mr A because he is a respected elder of the village; and we will never agree in public with Mr B because of the harm his grandfather did to our grandfather before the last war. A few newcomers might be welcome, a larger number makes us uneasy and a whole horde becomes a threat to our way of life. However many or few come, we take our time getting to know them. We may not go to church all that often, but it is our church because it has been passed down by our ancestors. It may be freezing in winter but we wrap up well and arrive at the last minute and get home quickly for our coffee (and perhaps a brandy too).

The newcomers, the mobile people, bring quite different assumptions about the nature of community life. For them it is generally much more straightforwardly commercial. If Mr B is a good workman and his prices are right, we will employ him in preference to Mr A, who seems both old-fashioned and expensive. We agree or disagree according to the sense another speaks; he may have been the boss of the steel works or the head of the local school but nonsense is still nonsense. If the church is going to hold us it needs to be a friendly and welcoming place (physical warmth is part of being welcoming these days; it's not just the people!). We make judgements about others fairly quickly and may not give ourselves time to discover that the quiet old man in the corner has a wicked sense of humour, or that the shy young woman has a heart of gold.

What is the balance between the newcomers and the long-established settlers if this is a distinction you recognize in your local church? Which group is dominant? Whichever community dominates the church will naturally have a character which tends to favour that community at the expense of the other; if it is possible to negotiate a compromise between the two communities, so much the better. This is not easy to do, and we shall look more closely at what it might involve shortly, but it is important to recognize that professional clergy tend to be mobile people rather than settlers. When they first arrive in a local church they are certainly seen as 'new' and are likely to be biased toward all that goes with mobility, though it is quite likely that the settlers will make a serious bid to win them over to their point of view.

Collective decision making

One of the shifts in our shared patterns of behaviour that I sense is testing traditional patterns of being church is the extent to which we all now expect to be involved in serious decisions. This is not a universal phenomenon, but I sense that an important transition is being made which can be expressed in schematic terms like this:

1 Some time ago clergy made all the significant decisions themselves. (This may not have been as radical as it sounds, because the rate of social change was slower and there were not so many decisions to make. The basic pattern was 'same again'.)

2 A good while ago now the practice began of electing lay people to share in making significant church decisions. The initiative for change – the suggestion of the need for a significant decision – still usually came from the clergy, but the lay people had the power to endorse or reject the suggestion. An adversarial pattern of decision making developed in many places – modelled perhaps on Parliament with its loyal opposition – whereby one or other party was seen as the 'winner'. A serious drawback in this system eventually emerged, which became evident whenever proposals for development were

rejected and no further proposals or suggestions were forthcoming. The pattern then favoured the status quo, because significant change seemed possible only at the cost of major disagreement. A stalemate resulted because the cost of suggesting change seemed too high.

3 A new pattern is now emerging where the responsibility for development is recognized as belonging to all (the whole body of Christ) and the suggestions for development are worked out by everyone at cooperative rather than confrontational meetings. There may still be arguments and very disappointed people, but the nature of the process used to make these decisions helps people become reconciled to not getting their preferred course of action.

Democracy, in the sense of sharing responsibility for major decisions affecting the life of a local church, does not apply simply to the freedom to accept or reject a proposal. It means involvement in shaping the proposal itself, which includes among other things being able to contribute to the dialogue about the advantages and the drawbacks of any proposed changes.

This shift is coming about in voluntary communities like churches because a larger proportion of people recognize the enormous importance of *participating* in the communities we belong to. In the past many people felt they had no say about the nature of the communities they belonged to; because of a widespread desire to conform and the lack of alternatives, they fell in with the ways of those communities. Now that we are better educated and more confident about the value of our own views, less inclined to accept the opinion of so-called *experts* or professionals, we question almost everything. If this questioning is rebuffed or evaded then we have the freedom to walk away. And we do this, not merely out of pique because we personally have not been taken seriously, but because we know deep down that the kind of Christian community we are called to be part of is best constructed by the active participation of all its members. This is the radical meaning of collaborative ministry. Of course there will be very young and very old members and others who cannot or do not wish to take a part in this process, but at the heart of a healthy church will be members who are active participants, sharing responsibility for its common life.

This means that it is important to find a way for the questioning and contributing to happen in a wholesome and productive fashion.

The moral and ethical context

Many people feel that the contemporary moral context is becoming more and more difficult. It is changing, certainly, but different is not necessarily worse. One of the ongoing tasks of the church is to reinterpret the nature and significance of holiness and sin. In today's world much of this revolves around the acceptance of one another.

The holy God, and therefore the holy person and the holy community, accept people as they are. This element of moral theology is felt to be an expression of the Christian gospel of unconditional love. It also seems to have a clear logic: God made people what they are, so God will accept them as they are. Sin is to reject people, for whatever reason.

This is not a moral standpoint that is argued for on the basis of specific biblical texts, though it does seem to many people to reflect Jesus' attitude toward the people he met and accepted as they were. But whether it accords with Jesus or not, many people feel it is axiomatic for good relationships between people.

So the prevailing mood suggests that we should accept people as they are – regardless of the colour of their skin, the language they speak, the religion they follow, their sexual orientation, their gender, their nationality, their intelligence; indeed almost any distinguishing feature we can think of. This grand ideal is, like all grand ideals, impossible to practise consistently. It naively relies on a reciprocity which is not always there – can I accept your religion if you will not accept mine? And it assumes that we are capable of a generosity and openness which ignores the psychological make-up of most people. But for all its obvious inadequacies it is there as a guiding conviction for many people, within the church and without. People approach the church today expecting the response to be Yes. It presents us with many challenges.

It is in fact a great starting point for peacemaking, for dialogue and for improving mutual understanding, but it can also seem to trap us into becoming what Dietrich Bonhoeffer might call peddlers of cheap grace, as if being accepted as you are means that God is entirely satisfied with us just as we are. It is certainly a great improvement on the assumption that the church was going to be condemnatory and censorious, but it can lure us into being wishy-washy, blessing almost everything.

Acceptance and rejection

The Bible offers many examples of the struggle about who can be accepted and who has to be rejected. Abraham argues with God about the number of innocent or upright or righteous people needed to prevent the destruction of everyone in Sodom and Gomorrah (Genesis 18.16–33). Abraham does not receive a numerical answer and Sodom and Gomorrah are destroyed, but he has been listened to. The New Testament contains evidence of the decisive turning point whereby circumcision (being Jewish) was rejected as an essential condition for becoming a Christian.

Whenever we meet someone new a process of mutual assessment takes place. It is natural and unavoidable, very complex and enormously important. When someone new comes into church, the basic pair of questions implicit in the situation is:

Are you going to welcome me?
Are you the sort we want to welcome?

These questions are instinctive, and are answered almost immediately on the basis of first impressions. The answers are conveyed as much by manner as by any words spoken.

Acceptance is perhaps the single most important criterion for belonging to a church. Will the church accept me as I am and will I accept the church as it is? The two-sidedness of the question is important and is often overlooked. If I am a hesitant, shy person I will be much more sensitive to whether people accept me, but if I am a bold, confident type I am more likely to be sensitive to whether the church is the kind of community I can accept.

Communication with one another in the present context

One paradox of the modern world with all its advanced methods of communication is that new technologies can divide us almost as much as we are brought together. In part it is a matter of having the technology in the first place; without a computer you cannot go to the website! But even with a computer or a mobile phone you can be overwhelmed by the multitude of possibilities. Confidence with new technology divides the generations – even the joke 'We had the children so they would work the video recorder' is out of date – but there are members of every generation who are very familiar with all the latest possibilities as well as some who want nothing at all to do with it. To what extent the local church uses such possibilities will depend on its resources; it is certainly an important area for Christians to explore and learn to use.

But one thing the local church has to offer which is free of all technological aids is face-to-face contact with other people. This is an enormously valuable gift we are in danger of overlooking. It is surprising how many people live alone and have few contacts with other human beings; it is this ordinary face-to-face human contact and companionship which the local church can and often does offer to the wider community.

Companionship and coffee

Several churches I know have developed simple regular coffee mornings – sometimes known as CAMEO mornings, which stands for Come And Meet Each Other – which enable this kind of face-to-face contact. If you go for a coffee on your own in a typical coffee shop you don't often join in conversation with others, but at a CAMEO morning you expect to talk to strangers and expect them to talk to you. The companionship and the conversation are more valuable than the coffee!

Ourselves as experts

There will almost certainly be other factors which both make your church unique, and present it with unique challenges and unique opportunities. One of the significant lessons many organizations are learning as they contemplate this uniqueness is that they cannot rely on the expert advice of people who have been here before and already developed the skills and insights that are needed. Instead we need to recognize that we ourselves are the people who know our own situation best and so we have to become our own experts. This is coupled with the realization that the ideas and the enthusiasm for development are already present among us. What is needed is a way of discovering and empowering this feature of congregational life. I have already referred to Open Space Technology in Chapter 6, but in Part 2 of this book we will look at the possibilities which this and other large group methods offer as part of the way of working with the wisdom of the congregation.

Summary

If as a local church you have engaged with all the themes of these seven chapters, what might you expect to have discovered?

In terms of the **mirrors**, we will probably have discovered several things about ourselves which we may not have noticed before. But whether the 'reflections' are already familiar or not, the important thing is that they are recognized as our own. No external person has insisted that that is what we look like. Admittedly the framework for each reflection may have seemed new or even contrived (by framework I mean the four purposes, sizes or outlooks, or the stages of the life cycle), but given the framework, the response we have given is all our own work. We can ask, Have we got ourselves right? but we cannot say someone else has misjudged us. This is significant for several reasons.

First, it points to our own shared responsibility for who we are, which in turn points to our shared responsibility for our own development. The different frameworks make the implicit point that there is more than one way of being a local church – there are other possibilities which we might have chosen. These alternative possibilities can stand as a challenge to the particular choice we ourselves have made (just as our choice stands as a challenge to other local churches who have made different choices).

Second, discovering this together, especially when we have discovered what I have called a shared predicament – like being in a size transition or trying to hold three purposes in equal balance – can help us see more clearly the nature of some of the tensions or frustrations we may have been experiencing. In particular it helps us see that many of these things are not due to any one person's or party's fault; they arise from our mutuality – how we are together – and can only be resolved on that basis.

Third, because it is a shared account and not one person's view, it may be a way for everyone to learn things they didn't know before. This can happen quite clearly as we recount the church's story; we might have discovered half-known events from the past which still influence the shared attitude or policy. But it can also happen more subtly, when we as individuals (especially if we are the minister) learn that our assumptions and convictions about the purpose of the church, for example, are not shared by the majority.

The **health check** points to a number of features which may unfortunately be quite difficult to assess. Just as with our physical bodies the same symptom – a pain in the stomach, for example – may have a range of possible causes, some much more serious than others, which cannot be determined without further investigations, so the simple discovery of warning symptoms may or may not suggest that radical 'treatment' is needed. Similarly, one symptom can distort or disguise another. Some local churches do find themselves suffering from quite serious conditions which call for careful and thoughtful treatment, though it is beyond the scope of this book to offer this in any detail. The main advice, if you feel this applies to you, is to ask for help. One debilitating malady is to feel that we can always cure ourselves!

In the terms of the themes we have considered in Chapters 1 to 6, my experience suggests that the following conditions present significant health challenges:

- a major trauma in the recent past
- a size transition between medium and large, especially if 'burnout' is present or suspected

- three major purposes with equal support (a 30:30:30 church)
- an agreed position well into the downward slope of the life cycle.

Perhaps slightly less challenging but still worthy of serious attention are:

- local churches with a 'golden age' in the not too distant past
- churches trying to give equal support to two major purposes (40:40 churches)
- churches that place themselves at the beginning of the downward slope of the life cycle where a few people – the aristocrats – make all the key decisions
- churches where the leadership – especially the ordained minister – has an opposite outlook to the majority of the congregation.

The challenge is all the greater if two or more of these features are present together.

Thanks to the operation of a very unhelpful logic, many people are inhibited from looking for appropriate help:

- we feel this sort of thing ought not to happen in Christian churches;
- because it ought not to happen we make no provision for meeting it if it should happen;
- therefore (almost as a policy) we have no idea what to do, so we try to carry on as if nothing had happened.

This may seem an unfair caricature, but it is uncomfortably near the truth in some cases.

What is needed in such cases – to stay within the health metaphor – is a small 'medicine chest' containing various remedies. These might include:

- using the self-awareness exercises in this book to see whether they help us understand – and by implication, do something about – the reasons underlying our distress;
- inviting an experienced 'outsider' in the form of a consultant, or, in the absence of an ordained minister, appointing an interim minister to help with the necessary treatment;
- asking for help in mediation and conciliation;
- in mild cases, searching the literature about resolving conflict in churches.

The building up of such a medicine chest has a number of wider implications. At the level of our denominations and local associations we need to search for and train people with the skill and aptitude to be of help to congregations in this sort of mess. Not only will they be very helpful; their very existence – if it is advertised – will help local churches recognize that many of us do face such crises from time to time and need outside help.

Examining the local church via the perspective of **building design** can help us recognize that we can design (and redesign) the way we organize our life together; there is rarely only one way of doing things. Where size is concerned, for example, we may see that a particular way of organizing church life works well for a medium-size church but presents considerable problems if it is used as a model for churches which are significantly larger or smaller. One size does not fit all, and one organizational structure will not serve a multitude of purposes.

As I have already pointed out, the frameworks I have used for the questions you have been invited to answer in the first six chapters have themselves provided alternatives with implications for the design or organizational structure of your common life. There is not one best way of organizing a Christian church, but there are better and worse ways of organizing, appropriate to your purposes, resources and circumstances.

Different purposes and different outlooks, like different people with different gifts and different needs, have implications for the way we design the organizational structures of our local church. Some of the reflective work suggested in the preceding chapters will have pointed to the implications of this, such as, for example, the contrasts that we recognized between the demands on members of a church dominated by the purpose of providing worship within a fellowship of mutual support (belonging and taking part) and one setting out to provide worship and service to the wider community (volunteering and net-working in the community), which demand contrasting organizational structures.

The perspective of **practical wisdom** will be the major theme of Part 2 of this book. Here, by way of introduction, I mention just a few convictions of mine about wisdom:

- Becoming as aware as we can of our own practical wisdom is an essential part of wisdom.
- Our practical wisdom, when it works well, holds together all the competing 'wisdoms' which we bring to our common life.
- Practical wisdom is aware of the possibility and usually the need to become wiser still.
- The best development for a local church is the development of its own God-given wisdom.
- We become wiser by making decisions and reflecting on their consequences.

***

We would love to rest *in your eternal changelessness*, Lord,
but it is hard to do in this rapidly changing world.
For example,
What would Jesus have made of modern media?
Would he have had his own television show –
even his own mass media company?
Kept an online blog, used Facebook and Twitter?

We just don't know.
Some of his present-day disciples see enormous opportunities in
these developments.
Others prefer just a modest involvement,
while a few have no interest at all in these new-fangled things.

But it's not only the technology, the mood is changing.
If we expected the clergy to make all the decisions in the past,
we are not happy with that now.
Everyone expects the church to be accepting of all sorts of things
these days, as if you, Lord, are simply an indulgent Heavenly Father
who has lost the capacity to be offended.

How do we make our way through this changing territory?
Should we listen more carefully to what the general public want?
Is imaginative marketing the way forward?
Your kingdom come, your will be done,
but what part do we play in the answering of that prayer, Lord?

Part 2

WORKING WITH OUR PRACTICAL WISDOM

8

Wisdom and development
Genuine wisdom is always ready to learn

Every local church is unique; no other church has its particular combination of traditions, stories, buildings, circumstances, resources and challenges. And yet each church will share many characteristics with other local churches. The six themes we explored in Part 1 – together with all the other factors we have only been able to hint at – will have gone some way toward enabling you to describe the uniqueness of your own church, while at the same time relating it to features and predicaments which are common to many churches.

The uniqueness of every local church means that development for one church will not be the same thing as development for another. Wholesome development has to be appropriate to a church's uniqueness. This poses a problem for a book that is supposed to be about the development of the local church – what can you say that will be appropriate for all?

My answer is that we do this by *working with the wisdom of the congregation*, the practical wisdom that we discovered in Part 1. The heart of wholesome development is the development of our shared wisdom. The mirrors into which we have looked, the health checks we have undergone, the building plans we have had drawn up have given us some idea of the wisdom we already possess, the way we do things in our particular church, a better understanding of ourselves than we had before.

Working with the wisdom of the congregation, the body of Christ, in the particular place where we are is a vital way of recognizing our uniqueness and acknowledging the limitations of experts. Or, to put it another way, it is to recognize that we, as a congregation, need to acknowledge our own expertise in these matters.

What exactly is our wisdom? It is not something that can be readily captured by words, like a definition in a dictionary. It is a mixed bundle of what we take for granted, what we usually do, the advice we give ourselves, the reflecting we do in the light of events, our thinking, our responses to people and situations, our convictions and our willingness to learn.

Wisdom, laws, theories and narratives

One characteristic of wisdom, when we do try to put it into words, is that it tends to be expressed as a set of proverbs, maxims or theses which point to patterns of both behaviour and thinking – to policies, rather than to laws or theories or narratives. This is a tricky distinction to suggest because there is certainly a very important kind of wisdom expressed in laws, theories and narratives. But the wisdom I am trying to point to has a restlessness, a seeking and questioning nature that is not so characteristic of the other three.

Laws, theories and narratives

Laws set out what we may and may not do. They regulate behaviour and ideally they do this in a clear and unambiguous way; they concern themselves with agreed limits for our actions. They serve a very important role in defining what is acceptable and unacceptable in social behaviour. They represent a kind of condensed wisdom about the conditions for living happily together.

Theories, on the other hand, seek to hold together a variety of phenomena in a way that explains them and enables us to predict what is likely to happen. So gravitational theory explains and predicts the movement of planets and tides, and much else besides, and in a different way a theory of water-borne diseases enables us to explain and predict the spread of cholera. Such theories can of course be wrong: one terrible so-called theory suggests that a man suffering from HIV & AIDS might be cured by having sexual intercourse with a virgin. Theories nevertheless present themselves as facts, often very complex facts, which can be relied on.

Narratives link together events and circumstances in the lives of individuals and communities which provide an important account of the complexity of who we or they are. Every narrative is also an interpretation of what has happened. It is often the case that different people involved in what seems like the same event will relate it in quite different ways. We considered in Chapter 1 the rival versions of the sale of the grand old rectory and its replacement by a modern house – an event regarded by some as a sensible step and by others as a great mistake.

Wisdom, I want to suggest, respects laws, theories and narratives and yet it gives prominence to two very significant things over and above these: the need to question, and the need to see that there is an elusive factor which laws, theories and narratives by themselves will never provide.

The need to question

The need to question is built into the wisdom of law, theory and narrative. As the world changes and new phenomena like the internet arise, new laws are required in order to police them, while old patterns of punishment come to be seen as ineffective or even barbaric. Simple theories which may have seemed self-evident – such as the idea that the use of modern language and modern music will attract and hold the younger generation – may need to be modified or even rejected in the light of evidence. And many narratives which have been told and retold can be seen to embody and reinforce assumptions and attitudes, such as patriarchy or racism, which we now want to leave behind. This is not to question the adequacy of law, theory or narrative in general, but to question the adequacy of particular laws, theories or narratives. Some theologians speak of the hermeneutic of suspicion which needs to be applied to many of the things we take for granted.

Wisdom recognizes the importance of questioning. Wisdom recognizes too that we cannot be forever questioning. We have to move on, we have to live our lives on the basis of the wisdom we presently enjoy, aware that some of the things we reckon are wise and good may well turn out to be foolish. But we cannot know that in advance; we only discover it as we live lives based on our present wisdom while at the same time making room for questioning and reflection, the deeper aspects of lifelong learning.

The elusive factor

But wisdom is more than that, certainly Christian wisdom should be. It involves the joyful recognition that there are values, possibilities, heights and depths to life that may always be elusive but are worth striving for. If we were to make a list of such things I'm sure it would be much like St Paul's list of the fruits of the spirit in Galatians 5.22: 'love, joy, peace, patience, kindness, goodness, fidelity, gentleness and self-control'. Or we might focus on love, recognizing the prime place it has in the teaching and example of Jesus. Again, we might prefer a slightly less obvious candidate like communion, which draws attention to the nature of God as Holy Trinity and the church as a communion of saints.

I think myself that each of these points in the same important direction; emphasizing the work of the spirit will resonate more with some, while emphasis on love will probably not be contested but runs the risk of concealing by its familiarity love's deeper and challenging nature. Communion has the small advantage of being less familiar, so we may learn more by enquiring about the nature of communion with God and communion with one another. (The communion of saints includes our communion with those who have gone before us in the Christian life, but it also includes contemporary Christians, and not just exemplary ones; it includes you and me and all the other members of the congregation we belong to.)

Starting with our own wisdom

I hope it is clear that I don't mean to suggest that the congregational wisdom we have discovered in Part 1 of this book is perfect or ideal. The great thing about wisdom is that it freely admits the desirability of becoming wiser still. But our present wisdom is necessarily our starting point, even when it may seem clearly inadequate to some. The rest of this chapter will focus on the way wisdom can become yet wiser, emphasizing its questioning nature and its quest for the elusive gifts of the spirit, and for love, and for communion.

Wisdom questions itself and questions other wisdoms in its quest to become not just wiser but to share life in the spirit, in love and communion. Part of being wise is finding a wholesome balance between competing claims, especially between the competing claims of good things. We looked at this briefly when we discussed the purposes of the local church in Chapter 3. This kind of balance is something that each person and each congregation needs to work at for themselves. It needs regular attention; the balance that worked well yesterday may not be right for today with its shifting demands and new circumstances. But rather than focus on the very important idea of balance, I want to discuss the questioning wisdom does in terms of negotiations. I am going to do this by discussing our wisdom's negotiations with several separate things, though in reality these are usually all muddled up together. I have divided these negotiations into two broad unscientific categories: obvious things and less obvious things.

My list of obvious things includes Scripture, traditions, organizational structures, other wisdoms, practicalities, limitations and consequences.

My list of less obvious things includes private meaning and collective meaning (I shall explain these terms when we get to them), distance, and challenging behaviour: evasion, aggression, stupidity, impatience and other enemies of love.

Negotiating our wisdom with obvious things

Negotiating with Scripture

The Bible plays such a central part in our worship and thinking as Christians that it may seem odd to suggest that we are in some kind of negotiation with Scripture. Our relationship with the Bible is very complex both as individuals and as congregations. This is because both the Bible and we ourselves are very rich and complicated. We may make statements in all sincerity about the authority of the Bible but find ourselves preferring some passages and studiously ignoring others.

This picking and choosing – which I believe everybody does – is part of what I mean by negotiation. It happens because we are not wholly rational beings, a fact about you and me which I believe to be enormously important and far from lamentable. Very few of us read or listen to Scripture being read and treat it as a set of instructions for life, similar to the instructions for assembling the kind of furniture which comes in a flat pack. Sometimes – but not invariably and probably not all that often – a passage of Scripture will speak directly to us and make a profound impression, even determining the course of our life from then on. But more often we read or hear a passage of Scripture, and by the end of the day we cannot remember anything at all about it.

Some Scripture passages resonate: they ring bells, challenge, inspire, accuse or comfort us. Other passages go over our heads, we don't know what they are about or they are about matters which are of no interest to us.

The lectionary which most local churches follow for their Scripture readings Sunday by Sunday has already edited the Bible, leaving out the passages which would seem to be too obscure or irrelevant or unedifying for public reading, or just because to include everything would make the readings far too long. This is a negotiation with Scripture which I think is wise and sensible, even if I might quibble with some of the details. And those churches which do not follow an agreed lectionary are inevitably making a selection of their own.

Regular reading of Scripture, usually taken up and expounded in sermons, is a normal feature of the life of most local churches. It reminds us of the basic biblical stories, teachings, exhortations and warnings, and shapes who we are as a congregation. But it does this in a general way. The Bible does not refer directly and obviously to many of the challenges that face us today, for example, how to adapt as a congregation to significant growth or decline, what to do about historic church

121

buildings, recognizing that a particular local church ought to join forces with another, and so on. Negotiation with Scripture happens at another level, concerning what we might call the scriptural principles which play a part in our thinking and deciding; principles that include generosity, forgiveness, humility and listening to what the spirit is saying to the churches. Developing our wisdom in negotiation with Scripture is a vital ingredient for Christian wisdom, even though it is impossible to pin down exactly how it comes about.

Negotiating with traditions and structures

Another obvious negotiation takes place with traditions and structures we have inherited. We do not and cannot start with the equivalent of a blank sheet of paper. The vast majority of local churches belong to a tradition (including a denomination) which gives shape and structure to who they are. Many churches belong to a worldwide or nationwide body which gives them legitimacy and offers support and discipline. Others belong to a network of likeminded churches, while retaining a high degree of individual autonomy. Some have a clear hierarchy of ministry; others have a different way of organizing themselves. Broadly speaking each congregation will feel that such structures as it has inherited or chosen to follow, are right and proper. This is the starting point for our practical wisdom about such matters. But most people also acknowledge that every tradition has its strengths and weaknesses. It may be very good for one purpose, but it is not so good at another – the traditional church council may be very good at dealing with routine business but is not so good at imaginative thinking or developing a strategy. Sometimes we may be convinced that these strengths and weaknesses belong inescapably to the tradition; at other times we may feel that it is not so much the traditional structure as the way it is operated and interpreted that is crucial.

So, for example, a particular body like the Bishop or Conference may have full authority within our tradition to make some vital decisions, and we do not basically object to that. But if those decisions are made without consultation or regard to the people who will be most affected by them, we feel badly treated. Wisdom will seek to negotiate the best ways of working the tradition. Successful negotiations are often called 'best practice', and that is a good description, as long as we recognize that best practice in one local church may not be identical with best practice in another. Wisdom questions the traditional structures about how each church can best fulfil its important organizational functions and at the same time build up the body of Christ.

Placing the shared wisdom of the congregation, the body of Christ, at the centre of attention (in contrast, say, to trying to develop the wisdom of the clergy) makes a significant contribution to this kind of negotiation. Being able to make important decisions as a congregation is a very important part of our dignity; it makes a vital contribution to building up the body. When other people make decisions we could and should have made ourselves, we are weakened as a community.

The relation between clergy and congregation is traditionally depicted as being analogous to that of shepherd and sheep. Yet this metaphor is not always a happy one, even though it has biblical origins. In the past this may have seemed the most sensible way to organize church life, but a wise questioning of the tradition shows that most Christians today are not content to be treated as sheep, and with good reason.

Congregations and flocks of sheep

Perhaps congregations never have been happy to be treated as sheep.

In his book entitled *You Wretched Corinthians*, the German pastor Hans Frör sets out an imagined correspondence between St Paul and members of the Corinthian church, based on the Corinthian Epistles in the New Testament and a great deal of careful study. He captures, it seems to me, the kind of intense dialogue that a wisdom negotiation involves. It is not at all a matter of courteous attention being paid to the apostle, as if he were a learned and distinguished professor dispensing wisdom for the church members gratefully to soak up. It is much more of a passionate argument – Why do you say that? Are you sure that is how Christians should behave? Have you thought about the consequences for women? Or for slaves? And how honest are you being with us? Do we scare you? Don't you realize that Corinthians are not exactly like the people of Jerusalem, or Ephesus for that matter? We have our own ways of doing things, our own traditions and values!

What we have here is passionate engagement, not quiet submission to the authority even of an apostle. It engages heart and mind because it is about souls and bodies and not just ideas. It is the kind of encounter that develops wisdom.

Negotiating with other wisdoms

Another set of negotiations takes place with what I call 'other wisdoms'. These are genuine wisdoms, appropriate in their original contexts, but less appropriate if transferred without adjustment to the life of a particular local church. I have in mind the wisdoms of accountants, managers, teachers, academics, politicians, lawyers, doctors, officers in the armed forces and salespeople, among others. Whatever can I mean by that?

Every profession has its own wisdom; indeed the very notion of a profession involves the development, integrity and protection of its own distinctive way of going about what it does. But such wisdoms are not readily transferable, certainly not in a simple sense, to the wisdom of a congregation. This is not to say that such professions do not have important things to offer a local church; only that these wisdoms need to negotiate their contribution with the shared wisdom of a Christian congregation. From the perspective of the balance that is such an important feature of wisdom, one danger is that such a wisdom should dominate while another is that it should be undervalued.

The following are a few examples of situations where such negotiations may be necessary:

- An accountant who professionally advises clients about legitimate ways of avoiding tax, organizes the presentation of the local church income in such a way that it radically minimizes the contribution that church makes to central funds (because the way contributions are calculated looks just like taxation). This policy works to the advantage of the local church in the short term, but severely limits what the central funds can do, part of which involves substantial support for the same local church. In the longer term, widespread adoption of this policy would be self-defeating. For one thing, it tends to alienate neighbouring churches who suspect that this church is not playing fair. For another, Scripture would suggest that simple generosity and the spirit of mutual responsibility and interdependence might temper the wisdom of tax avoidance. Changing such a policy will involve negotiation with the accountant, which may be complicated by the impression that in doing so, the congregation is questioning his or her professional competence (and maybe also his or her ethics).

- A manager who is used to the highly efficient organization of his business by means of clear schedules, job descriptions and rotas (including the sacking of inefficient workers) volunteers to do the same for the local church, and is dismayed to discover that such an approach is deeply resented. A negotiation between efficiency and the values of patience, forbearance, love and communion has to take place if there is not to be mutual rejection.

- People who have a significant academic training, which includes many clergy and those who preach, sometimes import the wisdom of rigorous argument and learned references into talks and addresses which effectively make them inaccessible. To quote Mary Butterworth (an ordinary saint of fond memory), 'He was very, very clever – he would tell us the meaning of Greek and Hebrew words. I don't think I ever understood a word he said!'

- The traditional wisdom of many local churches can be in danger of missing completely opportunities made possible by new technology, particularly in the field of communication. Learning to use such new opportunities will need to draw on the expertise of professionals. Very often this is also a challenge for different generations, younger people being much more familiar with methods which seem completely mysterious, and perhaps unnecessary, to older folk.

This negotiation of one wisdom tradition with another is often particularly crucial for the health of local churches. Although there is a natural tendency to value the wisdom of professionals over that of supposedly ordinary people, there is also a resistance. This can be fairly obvious when highly competent professionals move into a new area and join the local church, generously offering their skills without being aware that such generosity (from their point of view) can seem like implicit criticism of the congregation's own wisdom, and look like a threatening takeover bid.

Less obvious is the establishment of a group of wise men and women (almost always professionals) charged with making recommendations about the future of one or more local churches. This follows a venerable wisdom tradition (which is indispensable in many situations), whereby representatives listen, consult, deliberate and make recommendations, without at the same time seeking to persuade and educate those who will be most affected by their recommendations. So eminently sensible proposals are often resented and rejected, mainly because those most involved were not included in the process of decision making.

In this respect I think things in churches are changing. The deference that people generally gave to professional wisdom (a form of authority) is not what it used to be. In part this is because many people feel that the professional viewpoint is not the only way of looking at an issue; in part because they feel entitled to have a say, and to be persuaded about things which affect them; and in part because building up the body of Christ, strengthening the Christian community, is a mutual and shared responsibility. The emphasis I place on working with the wisdom of the congregation (as opposed to imposing professional wisdom on the congregation) is a recognition of this shared responsibility and a move away from the kind of

A resource for making choices

In my *Workbook for Developing the Local Church*, I have suggested a learning process for making good decisions in local churches. It involves nine steps, and it will seem unduly fussy to many people who see themselves as decisive leaders, but it is deliberately designed to slow the process down so that everyone concerned can learn about the complexities involved, and see that the process has been thorough and careful. The participants are required to spell out the issues and choices themselves; they engage in the necessary research, they contemplate the pros and cons of the different options, they make the decision and see it through.

The nine steps cover three phases, and there are three steps to each phase:

Phase 1   Diagnosing the situation
Step 1 Describing the situation as we see it
Step 2 Describing what we would like the situation to be
Step 3 Checking important things, including
- our purposes
- things we want to avoid
- consistency with our beliefs
- the resources to hand
- the needs to be met.

Phase 2   Exploring possibilities
Step 4 Clarifying our priorities
Step 5 Narrowing down our options and thinking through what each would involve
Step 6 Making a (provisional) choice

Phase 3   Careful implementation
Step 7 Checking the dimensions of the choice:
- Who else would be involved?
- What resources will be needed?
- How long would this take?
Step 8 Allocating the work in detail
Step 9 Implementing the work, celebrating the completion

This is an iterative process rather than an incremental one; this means you may discover that plans or assumptions made at one step have to be abandoned at a later stage, so you have to go back several steps and start again. The 'case' for the decision is built up

> through all the steps; it is clear that if Step 8 fails the choice made at Step 6 will not be implemented.
>
> The decision may be exactly the one a decisive leader would have made with much less bother, but the difference has to do with the development of the wisdom of the congregation. They have been taken seriously. It is this aspect of the process that contributes most to building up the body of Christ.

dependency which encourages immaturity. It is not that I as a layperson know better than you the professional; it is that I am a member of the community (congregation) whose future development is at stake and I am therefore entitled to be involved in the learning and deciding process.

One of the advances of recent years is the discovery of much more adequate ways of consultation and involvement than previous generations enjoyed, which are very valuable resources for the development of what is often called collaborative ministry.

Negotiating with practicalities and limitations

One of the perpetual negotiations for any kind of practical wisdom is with those matters that prove to be immovable and unpredictable. There may be all sorts of things we would love to do, which would be good to do, but which for one reason or another are impractical. One current example may be the practical impossibility of providing disabled access to our church. Wisdom has to accept that limitation in a positive way.

Negotiating with less obvious things

Negotiating with different kinds of meaning

One insight I have found very illuminating is that there are three broad kinds of meaning within any organization:

- private meanings
- collective meanings
- accessible meanings.

This distinction comes from Nancy Dixon's *The Organizational Learning Cycle: How We Can Learn Collectively*. Private meanings are those that are not made public, though they are often guessed at: 'I'm looking for a husband/wife'; 'This church will be a good stepping stone for promotion'; 'My role in the church gives me an importance I don't find anywhere else.' Collective meanings are those which we tend to take for granted; they are basic and not easily talked about, at least not within the church. They might include 'Church is good', 'The choir is essential', 'We need more ordained ministers.' Accessible meanings include the kind of things we have just been discussing, things that are open for discussion and negotiation.

Accessible meanings are just that: accessible to negotiation. Private and collective meanings may exert a powerful influence on what happens, almost without anyone realizing it or at least being prepared to talk about it. We sometimes warn each other 'Don't even think about it!', should there be a hint that someone is about to resign or that the pews are going to be removed, or even that a drum kit might be introduced!

Boundaries between accessible meanings and private and collective meanings are not clear and sharp. Part of their power lies in this lack of clarity. We are reluctant to broach certain topics for fear of causing offence; we are not sure but we think that a certain individual would be dreadfully upset if we made a particular suggestion. We find we have guessed at how that person would respond, which takes away from him or her some of the dignity of being taken seriously. It is also a fuzzy boundary that some people try to exploit, for it is an area abounding in rumour and innuendo. 'They are planning to close our church and sell the site!' 'If we do this, people will stop giving.' 'If that happens, I will leave the church!' No one knows how true these things are, whether some people are bluffing or not; perhaps the people themselves don't know for sure but feel it is a threat worth feeding into the grapevine.

Bringing meaning into the open

How does Christian practical wisdom engage with this? The most straightforward way is by bringing as much as possible into the area of accessible meaning. (Less straightforward ways include aggression and evasion: more on these later.) Your church's engagement with the six aspects of practical wisdom elaborated in Part 1 of this book will, if it has been undertaken seriously, already have provided some experience of arriving at shared conclusions. There has been no ulterior motive to the questions asked, and the way answers have been gathered has sought to minimize distortions due to any pressure to conform. This kind of anonymous opinion gathering, however, is not usually available for dealing with questions in the borderland between private and collective meanings, and accessible ones.

Sometimes questions have to be enticed or even dragged into the accessible meaning zone where they can be addressed in a mature way.

This always takes time. When a contentious matter – the removal of historic pews, for example, or the replacement of the ancient pipe organ with an electronic one – is broached for the first time, it may well produce quite a fierce reaction, designed to frighten people off (an aggressive response). It is probably wise to make a tactical retreat if that happens, but not to be put off completely. A second approach – after a space in which all involved have time to reflect – might seek not to reinstate the question so much as to discover why there is such strong feeling about it. This should be a courteous enquiry, genuinely trying to discover reasons which can be shared and appreciated and talked about. This in turn may enable a third (straightforward) approach to discuss the matter more calmly and discover together whether any proposed action is wise, even though it will clearly cause understandable pain for some, or whether the proposal ought to be dropped for reasons which everyone can appreciate.

This process best takes place in as large a forum as possible. Many local churches are led by a small group of people, part of whose responsibility is to determine what appears on the agenda of any larger decision-making body. It is frequently within such a group that contentious issues are squashed and never reach a wider forum (an evasive response that happens so quickly it is hardly noticed!). It may seem something of a paradox, but I suggest that part of the wisdom of such small leadership groups is to question the wisdom of their own judgements, not by indecision and hesitation, but by testing matters in the wider congregation. This is because an essential part of the health of a congregation consists in participation, not just in activities provided by others, but in the very process of decision making and shaping the nature of the community.

This is something local churches learn to do by doing it. And it takes time. The first attempt may not seem particularly successful, especially in a community where people have not been used to being consulted; but as people recognize the dignity of being asked, they generally respond well.

Negotiating with distance

Human relationships always include a significant element of negotiation, and this is particularly true for the relationship between an individual and the local church he or she attends. One aspect of this negotiation concerns distance: how close or otherwise you feel to the shared life of the congregation. Remembering the different purposes of churches we looked at in Chapter 3, we could say that those who appreciate the local church for providing opportunities for worship and education in the Christian faith, but who do not wish to be caught up in other

The problems of agreement

In his book, *The Abilene Paradox*, Jerry B. Harvey, a professor of business studies in the USA, claims that many organizations suffer more from problems due to agreement than from those caused by conflict. His title comes from a family incident involving an outing to Abilene (a town in Texas) which nobody wanted to make, but which happened because everyone presumed – without asking – that agreement had been reached. It was only afterwards – the outing having been a mild disaster – that everyone discovered that none of them wanted to go on the trip in the first place.

The incident serves as a parable for many organizations that find themselves doing things which hardly anybody thinks are sensible but which everyone presumes have everyone else's support, though nobody actually tests this by asking. (In Nancy Dixon's terms it has become part of the collective meaning; nobody has tried to bring it into the accessible meaning zone where it can be questioned.)

Although Harvey does not place special emphasis on the word 'wisdom', I think his book is essentially about practical wisdom in the life of commerce and learning. To my mind it is an outstanding example of practical theology written by someone who does not claim to be a theologian!

aspects of church life, are at a greater distance than those who see the church as a place also for the fellowship of mutual support. Those who prefer worship without any other involvement will resist attempts to involve them in all kinds of social or practical church activities, while those who attend for fellowship will feel neglected and left out if they are not encouraged and invited to join in. Different people look for different degrees of closeness or distance. It is not that closer is better; it is a matter of negotiating a distance which is appropriate and wise.

Negotiating with challenging behaviour

Another negotiation of the less obvious kind involves what we politely call 'challenging behaviour'. Most of us expect other people to be reasonable in the way they behave, especially within the life of the congregation. But from time to time this does not happen: people throw tantrums, they threaten resignations, they make unfounded accusations, they behave in what seem to us profoundly unchristian ways. And partly because we feel these things ought not to happen, we have no idea what to do when they do occur.

There is of course a procedure for the really serious matters. Criminality should involve the police, our child protection policy tells us what to do if we suspect abuse, employees should have a grievance and disciplinary procedure to follow. But there are instances that do not come under headings like these, though they can seriously threaten the well-being of the congregation. Sometimes unreasonable behaviour can be a symptom of serious illness, including breakdown and other forms of mental illness. Occasionally it is a matter of a personal meaning breaking through – a protest at being neglected, an attempt to assert power or to get our own way. Sometimes we in the majority have to face up to the fact that we may have provoked the behaviour – we didn't let someone know, we made decisions that properly were not ours to make, we forgot something which should have been obvious.

Wisdom does well to anticipate such occurrences, by which I mean be prepared to accept them as important interruptions to normal life which need serious attention. Grievance procedures in employment practice are precisely such an anticipation; they represent an attempt to think carefully about how to deal fairly with difficult matters before they arise, aware that heightened emotions will be involved which most of us find make wise decisions rather more difficult. I don't want to suggest that we draw up contracts for every voluntary activity in church life, but I think that some careful discussion of the general principles involved *before such an incident occurs* would help most congregations. Topics might include how to respond when office holders refuse to retire at the stipulated time, what to do if an office holder refuses to implement decisions taken by the council or appropriate authority, and how to respond to threats to resign which appear to be attempts to change an agreed policy or increase the person's power.

One modest resource which helps us make at least a considered response to challenging behaviour is the discipline of thinking of three possibilities. (These have already played a part in earlier discussions in this chapter.) The idea is to script alternative responses (or at least make notes that could be the basis of a script): one is aggressive, another evasive and the third is what I prefer to call straightforward.

An aggressive response is a counter-challenge, an accusation of bad faith, an insult or some other expression of indignation which ignores the substance of the challenge. An evasive response similarly ignores the challenge by a strategy of appearing not to respond at all, or by passing responsibility on to a third party (usually one who isn't readily available) or claiming that you have no power to alter things, or dismissing the challenge as due to somebody being awkward. A straightforward response is prepared to investigate the complaint (if that is the form in which the challenge presents itself), apologize if appropriate and seek reconciliation. Or it may simply involve a closer look at what is at stake. Whatever else this does, it takes the person seriously, which is at the heart of what is called for.

★★★

We would love to be wiser, Lord
(especially if this could happen with little effort on our part!).
Wisdom is such a precious possession,
the facility of knowing just what is needed,
freedom from serious mistakes,
an unerring instinct for the right balance between competing claims.

But perhaps wisdom is about more than just being right most of
    the time,
it's about love and the fruits of the spirit and communion as well.
Which means it's also about being wrong some of the time
and being forgiven and forgiving others when they are wrong.
It's about living together, about sharing, about taking part,
about a wisdom which belongs to a community
and not just to individuals (as if individuals existed alone!).

So we negotiate our wisdom with many important things:
the wisdom of Scripture, the wisdom of our church traditions,
the wisdom of the professions and the common sense of ordinary
    people.
Wisdom learns, and learns to learn.
It does not capitulate to alternative wisdoms,
nor does it despise them but learns
to take what is appropriate and make that its own.

Wisdom is aware that negotiating can be hard work,
for quite a lot of what makes up our current wisdom
is hidden within private meanings, and
some of it is never questioned because it seems so obvious.
And then sometimes we are negotiating with our own reluctance
to face challenges or make hard choices.
And occasionally we are up against plain wickedness and
tenacious stupidity, in ourselves as well as others.

This kind of wisdom, like *the mind of Christ,* or the Holy Spirit,
will always be ahead of us,
never ours to grasp and own
but always to be desired and sought
and prayed for.

9

Wisdom is a way of life
Creating conditions which encourage shared learning

Practical wisdom becomes wiser as a result of both action and reflection. Nancy Dixon believes this involves four stages in a cyclical process which she calls the organizational learning cycle: Act, Generate, Integrate, Interpret, Act, and so on. In this final chapter I set out a simplified version of this process for learning, which I believe comes to a focus when we make decisions.

The wisdom I have tried to draw attention to in this book is a way of life, a complex bundle of thoughts and practices, convictions and habits which seems self-evidently sensible and right to its owners. The wisdom of a local church is the bundle which might be labelled, 'How we do things here'. Development, for both individuals and churches, will involve changes in the make-up of the bundle, but not usually its complete reorganization.

These changes come about through a process of learning and decision making. The learning and decision making belong together; in this way the development of wisdom differs from the kind of education that is principally about acquiring more and more information. Sometimes the learning is forced on us by a drastic change of circumstance, like the sudden death of a vital member or by the discovery that our church building has become unsafe and has to be condemned. More often it is through a more gradual process as we realize that if we carry on the way we are, in a few years' time there will be hardly anyone attending our church, or we shall run out of money or we won't have enough ordained ministers to maintain the status quo.

Our first reaction to such situations is often paradoxical: we deny or at least strongly resist the need to learn. This may seem unwise – it usually is – but it needs to be dealt with wisely. One reason for our resistance is the implication that our present wisdom is failing us. It had served us so well up to now that its failure is hard to believe – 'But we have always done it this way and it always worked before!' It is akin to having our common sense criticized.

Another reason is because we might feel the answer is obvious – we just need more members, more clergy, more money, more faith, more commitment, more of the familiar ingredients. This preserves the old wisdom intact.

A third reason could be that in reality we are hoping that someone else will save us. The new minister, the youth worker, the professional fundraiser – someone like this will kiss our Sleeping Beauty back to vigorous life! Just occasionally it happens, but not often.

It is important to explore these reasons and reactions together with a degree of sympathy, but without collusion. It is not easy for any group of people to accept that they are facing a crisis which threatens, if not their future survival, then at least their flourishing, especially if they feel that they have done nothing particularly wrong. It is a hard predicament. The objection to these and similar reactions is not that they are incorrect, but that they do not go out to meet the challenge. We need to take time to explore our predicament and come to our own conclusions, and draw up our own plans for making progress.

But where are the resources for learning what we need, for developing our wisdom? There are no foolproof answers to such an important question, but I suggest that there are at least five areas where potentially fruitful explorations might be carried out:

- the retelling of stories
- the appropriate design of how we organize our common life
- the thoughtful matching of people and tasks
- the process of decision making
- the shared management of change.

The retelling of stories

In Chapter 1 we looked at the significance of the local church's story. Retelling the church's story is particularly suitable for a local church that senses its morale is low, or which is in danger of being complacent. There are several stages in the retelling of a congregation's story.

Acknowledging your story

The first is to acknowledge your story, share it and celebrate it. Many written church histories concentrate for the most part on what happened to the building and who the ministers were. They would be much richer if they recorded how the congregation responded to events like the death of Princess Diana, September 11, 2001 and the London bombings, as well as to more local events like the closure of a major industry, the loss of a local school or the influx of immigrants from Asia, and to social trends like the increasing demand for the baptism of babies whose parents have chosen not to marry.

Many churches have a patronal festival or mark the anniversary of their founding; such are obvious occasions for celebrating the church's story and filling out the detail in this kind of way. Adding to the church's time line with parallel time lines recording what was happening in the neighbourhood and in the wider world can be very interesting and illuminating.

Questioning your story

The second stage is to question the story, not in a condemnatory spirit but in an attempt to interpret it more adequately, and so retell it better. If you were able to do the work suggested in Chapter 1, you will have both a shape for your church story and an indication of the things you feel you are good at. Have you got this right? If you have a more or less downhill shape leading to the present, how do you interpret that? Is it an indication of failure, to be blamed on circumstances or deficient leadership, or a challenge (which ultimately comes from God) about who you are and how you live out the gospel? The interpretation of setbacks and failures is particularly important. A sense of being let down or unfairly treated, or of not being up to the task, carries the original wound into the present and colours our view of the future. On the other hand, is a shape of ordinary ups and downs an indication that we have been insulating ourselves from hard questions?

The insights gained from working through other chapters may illuminate the story in important ways. Our sense of frustration and working at cross-purposes may be better understood in terms of the size transition we are experiencing, or because we are trying to do things which rival each other for limited resources, or because we have reached a stage on the life cycle which implies a struggle between the generations. If we have discovered this kind of interpretation of our predicament by working together – with the very important freedom from assigning praise and blame – we are more likely to share ownership of the predicament and together attempt to negotiate a way forward.

The list of what we are good at can be usefully interrogated, not in the direction of downgrading but in terms of going deeper into what it implies. If we pride ourselves on being friendly and welcoming, is this simply reactive – being friendly and welcoming to those who come to us? Or might it be proactive, going out of our way to be friendly and welcoming to people who are unlikely ever to come to us unless we invite them and work hard at welcoming them? (I'm thinking of

Renaming and decision making

John Bell, in *The Singing Thing: A Case for Congregational Song*, writes (p. 103) about the sad way in which so many people believe they cannot sing because someone in authority long ago told them so. The remedy, he says, lies in renaming and decision making. He tells some encouraging stories of how people who believed for many years that they could not sing discovered the liberation and joy of song.

In a similar way I think that many congregations have been trapped in negative stories about themselves which need to be retold and decisively left behind. I recall learning of the 'worst meeting' some denominational officials had ever attended in a local church, after the previous minister had moved on. The meeting was supposed to be discussing the church's future, but there was so much anger that it was impossible to make any progress. It transpired that the minister had repeatedly told the congregation that the denomination would close the church down if he moved on, and sell the building and its land. He was apparently using this threat as an attempt to get his own way. The tactic failed, but the story was believed and the denominational officials unwittingly received the full blast of the church's indignation.

families who may have a member with special needs, for example, but there are many hidden groups within our communities who assume they would be a nuisance at a typical church service. Our invitation would in many cases be a liberating piece of good news, but only if we ourselves were prepared to make these people really welcome by accommodating what we normally do to their specific needs.)

The appropriate design for organizing our common life

This possibility is a little more technical, but not beyond the reach of most congregations. Some evidence of a need for it will have emerged as a result of the work you have done together already, and some ways forward have been indicated in the relevant chapters. Several possible reorganizations may be needed. They could relate to a size transition, to a certain mix of purposes (40:40 and 30:30:30, in the terms of Chapter 3) or to backtracking on the life cycle curve. Sometimes they are made more complicated by involving a bit of each!

I have two broad recommendations to make. One is that a sympathetic outsider can be a great help in this area. The other concerns a shared awareness of the inevitability of disagreement and rivalry in any congregation, which should be seen more as a sign of vitality than an indication of trouble.

Finding the right kind of outsider to help you can be a challenge in itself. The kind of person who knows just what you need *before* he or she has even met you is no real help at all. You are seeking to develop your wisdom, not extend the range of someone else's. You are looking for an enabler, a facilitator, someone who will help you understand the processes involved in organizing yourselves in ways that are appropriate to your size, your purposes, the stage of development you have reached and your context.

You can usually find such a person if you ask around, and some people can readily learn these skills. Most local churches have access to a network through which enquiries can be made: if there is a training department, that would be the obvious place to begin.

The second recommendation amounts to an acceptance that half the task is always present, whatever you do. You may have adapted the congregation's organizational structure in ways that make it much more appropriate and efficient than before, but that doesn't guarantee a trouble-free life. Misunderstandings, mistakes, failures and even sometimes deliberate mischief-making are regular features of life together. It is the shared responsibility of every member of the congregation to contribute to the good management of such matters. Many minor offences – not checking whether a clash of events might occur before making a booking, for example, or doing someone else's job before they have a chance to do it – can be dealt with by the people immediately involved with a mixture of humour, correction and forgiveness. Harder cases may need to be referred to the leadership, though often they are already involved. No one can say in advance how they should be dealt with; it becomes a test of our shared wisdom, and will be an answer to prayer certainly (though not always the answer we hoped for).

Maintaining the congregation's health

Even when such difficulties as those outlined above are overcome, if we consider our situation from the perspective of the health check employed in Part 1, we can see how it points to the importance of maintaining good health. Just as individuals are urged to take plenty of exercise, to eat five portions of fruit or fresh vegetables a day, not to smoke and to drink alcohol in moderation, so there may be a similar list of simple things to do which can help keep the local church healthy.

It would be a useful exercise for a congregation to draw up its own recommendations for healthy congregational life as a way of reviewing and reflecting on its own behaviour. A major contribution to the happiness of individuals and churches is made by the success – often hardly noticed – of having no major problems, due at least in part to a healthy lifestyle. We may discover if we carry out such an exercise that we do not often make opportunities for this kind of thinking together to happen. Annual church meetings are frequently conducted as business meetings, with a strong bias toward finance; of course finance needs careful management, but within the context of larger questions about our values and purposes as a local church. Undertaking such thinking together at an annual meeting might prove very refreshing.

Thoughtful matching of people and tasks

One difficulty which afflicts the life of many congregations (and other organizations as well) is when people are given or acquire tasks which they are not good at, or happy with. This can come about in various ways:

- There may be a common expectation that the priest or ordained minister should be the leader of the church, and therefore responsible for chairing major committees and decision-making bodies. But this may not be the minister's forte at all. (Clergy are traditionally trained to lead worship, to preach, teach and offer pastoral care, but not usually to chair meetings.)
- One church official may have done several tasks, some of which were not a basic part of the office itself but which the official acquired because they employed his or her particular skill or interest. The official's successor is then expected to take on these things in addition to his or her own official duties.
- Some people happily volunteer to do things for which they have hardly any talent.
- A few people who have made important suggestions are landed with the task of implementing them ('You suggested it – you do it!'). But their strength is with imaginative ideas, not practical implementation (see the box on Belbin, p. 142).
- Some people hang on to tasks which they once fulfilled with flair and imagination, but which they now merely perform in a perfunctory way.

How do we deal sensitively with difficulties like this? It is another test for the practical wisdom of the congregation. Frequently such mismatches are tolerated as a way of evading the challenge; we don't want to upset people. And anyway it's the job of the leadership! Well, yes, it may be, but often the leadership is as much caught up in these mismatches as anyone else.

We have already (in Chapter 5) referred to the wisdom expressed in church rules and regulations about time limits for certain office holders. It is not always right to follow these to the letter, but it is always wise to raise the question at the appropriate time, and agree together if an exception should be made. Some office holders – whether church-wardens, treasurers, elders or church secretaries – come to regard their position as more of a dignity than a job, and dare anyone to take it from them. This is usually damaging for their spiritual health, and for the health of the congregation. It can be a mild case of emotional blackmail (though it is not usually wise to accuse people of this, for that often only makes matters worse!). All church office holders should be aware that they are invited to serve by the local church as a whole (not usually by the minister alone) and for a specific period, which is in many cases for just a year at a time. You may recall that when we discussed the life cycle of congregations in Chapter 5 we spoke about decline being marked by aristocracy and bureaucracy – when the same people are appointed year in, year out to make the same basic decisions they made before. Use the annual meeting to ensure that some people retire and some new people are appointed; or if that is not possible, make sure the reasons why are understood and the implications (see Chapter 5) are acknowledged.

A group exercise

In addition to grasping this important annual opportunity, leadership teams and church councils might try the following exercise. (I don't think this lends itself to everyone in the congregation doing it at once.)

1 As a group, first collect words describing the skills and abilities which are valuable for the shared life of the congregation. Think of functions or contributions rather than offices or jobs: things like 'ability to listen', 'an encourager', 'approachable', 'able to chair a meeting', 'good at welcoming newcomers', 'a source of good ideas', 'artistic', and so on. These can be collected on a flip chart for all to see.

2 Next, give everyone present a set of blank cards, as many cards as there are people present. After careful thought – and probably some prayer as well – write your own name on the first card and write down three things you like doing or feel are gifts which you could offer in the service of the church, preferably using words from the chart. These are collected without anyone else seeing what you have written.

3 Then write everyone else's name on the remaining cards – one card per person – and write down three things you feel that the named person is good at.
4 Put all the cards, including the first set, together and shuffle them.
5 Then simply deal out to each member of the group the cards with his or her own name on them. Everyone will recognize their own card, but others need not know which one it is.

The first message everyone will receive is a personal affirmation of their giftedness. If other people discern in you gifts you did not recognize in yourself this may be encouraging, but it may be disappointing too (you may think you are obviously good at a particular task, but no one else seems to agree!).

When everyone has had a chance to digest the implications of their own cards, you all look at one another's. What you now have is the group's perception of each member's gifts, as they relate to the needs of the church. Several results might flow from this:

- You may discover that some people are doing things which hardly anybody thinks use their gifts to the best advantage. You might then change roles in a way that is liberating for everyone.
- You are quite likely to find that between you there are plenty of people with similar gifts and hardly anyone with others (see the box on Belbin, p. 142). For example, many churches have plenty of ideas people and comparatively few 'completers' (to use one of Belbin's labels). One symptom of this lack is the experience of mutual frustration within a team or organization. You all get cross with one another because things are never seen through to a conclusion, without realizing that each of you is expecting everyone else to see to it! There are two constructive possibilities: one is to go out and find someone with the gifts needed to fulfil the missing role, another is specifically to delegate the task to one of the present members. It is much easier to check with people that they have done what they said they were going to do if that is a job the team have asked you to do!
- You may discover a number of unexpected or unused gifts which in turn suggest an area for possible development.

A rather different challenge to the wisdom of churches and denominations can occur when an ordained minister is appointed to a local church. It is one of the sad features of church life that sometimes when an apparently good minister goes to an apparently good local church, everything goes wrong.

I think that the kind of reflections on a congregation's practical wisdom described above could prove a valuable resource for reducing

Belbin's insights

Many readers will have heard of Meredith Belbin's work on teams. Belbin's discoveries are to be found in his book, *Management Teams: Why they Succeed or Fail* (a shorter account of Belbin's analysis is provided by Charles Handy in *Understanding Voluntary Organizations*). Belbin studied the composition of teams in a wide variety of situations, and discovered – as a lot of people already knew! – that teams made up of 'the best people' were frequently not the best teams. Too many able people are tempted to think that their ability means they should be in charge. This means that they frequently get in one another's way, frustrating the work of the team and frustrating their colleagues. A balanced team needs ideas people, but it also needs practical people who can make the ideas work, as well as people who will support the team members' basic needs – for breaks as well as intensive work, for example. It also needs what Belbin calls a 'completer', someone whose role is to see that people actually do what they said they would do, and a chairperson to give shape and order to meetings (though not necessarily to be the 'boss').

This is a very valuable insight which can illuminate a great deal of church life. Clergy in particular might note two things: one is that the traditional expectations of what clergy should do, which often amounts to taking charge, may inhibit both their own strengths and those of other people. The second is that a team of people who are chosen because they will support what you want to do is likely to be as frustrating as a team of 'the best people'. You need people who will ask questions and challenge the received wisdom!

these unfortunate mismatches. We can also use the reflections in the mirrors – represented diagrammatically as a 'hall of mirrors', for example – to compare our experiences and priorities with those of a prospective minister, or with the characteristics of another local church with whom we might work more closely or even combine. This is not a mechanical method for making important decisions but a way of raising significant questions. When the experience and priorities of a prospective minister are represented diagrammatically and placed alongside our own hall of mirrors, questions naturally arise about how well we would 'fit'. Would we together be a good match, or a challenge to each other, the kind of relationship that could give rise to fruitful tension for both parties? Or would the differences between us predict major difficulties ahead?

The process of decision making

One of the most significant opportunities for developing the shared wisdom of a congregation occurs when a decision has to be made. The manner in which important decisions are made within and for a voluntary community like a congregation is as important as the content of the decisions themselves. This is because decision making is a learning experience, calling upon our shared responsibility, and this in turn is part of our dignity. When other people make decisions on our behalf but without us, we are to a certain extent diminished: we have not been allowed to join in sharing responsibility for what has been decided.

Sharing responsibility for a decision is not the same as getting our own way. We can take part in a negotiation about the best way forward and discover that all our suggestions prove to be impractical or fail to gain necessary support. We may be disappointed but we can recognize that we have been honourably defeated in a fair process. Good, healthy decision making for local churches involves respecting the dignity of all who will be affected by the decision, which means involving them as much as possible in the process.

One of the great enemies of such a process is a sense of urgency, coupled with the judgement that there isn't really any choice about what has to be done. Unfortunately, quite a lot of this urgency is due simply to a failure to address the problem when it first arose. Procrastination is a form of evasion, and it is widely employed by churches, with the eventual result that people feel bounced at the last minute into decisions they are not happy about. It is to the credit of many church bodies that attempts are now being made to involve their members in thinking ahead and asking hard questions about how we are going to organize ourselves, if, as seems likely, we are going to have significantly fewer resources in the future. The so-called Hezekiah syndrome is an irresponsible evasion. (King Hezekiah responded to the prophet Isaiah's warning of impending doom by saying '"The word of the LORD which you have spoken is good," for he was thinking to himself that peace and security would last out his lifetime', 2 Kings 20.19).

The other enemy – that there is no choice – is even more powerful. It may prove to be true, but it still needs to be understood and accepted, even if reluctantly. We need to learn this and not simply take someone else's word for it. A good open process of decision making and consultation enables this important kind of learning.

Resources for sharing in decisions

One of the significant advances of recent years has been the discovery or invention of successful ways of consulting and involving
large numbers of people in matters which concern them. (Previously
we relied on large numbers being represented by a few people who
spoke and decided for them.) These include a method of breaking
down a process into constituent parts and guiding people through
it – the pattern of decision making involving nine steps which is
outlined on pp. 126–7.

Another is Open Space Technology, explored in more detail on
p. 146, and a third is Future Search, a process suited especially to
developing a longer term strategy for a local church. The full version
of Future Search – which can be seen on <www.futuresearch.
net> – is probably too elaborate and time-consuming for most
local churches, but it is possible to gain much from a shortened
version. The logic of Future Search is relatively simple, consisting
of four steps:

1 a careful assessment of where you are (covered by completing
   the six themes explained in Part 1 of this book)
2 a sense of shared responsibility for development
3 a disciplined imagining of a desired future (as outlined below)
4 a careful planning of how you get to where you want to be.

Building on the self-awareness that your local church has discovered
by working through the six themes in Part 1 of this book, hold a
meeting at which all who come are divided into small 'mix max'
groups (groups with the maximum mixture of people, that is, none
consisting exclusively of clergy, women, old, young, and so on –
people are usually able to sort themselves out given this brief
explanation). The task of each group is to imagine what they would
like the church to be in three or five or so years' time – a reasonable but not overlong period of time. This imagining is disciplined
by reasonable predictions, for example about the availability of
clergy or the likely state of the building or the finances. The group
note their reflections as they go along. If the work already done on
the six themes has indicated a challenge such as a size transition
(Chapter 2), or a generational tension (Chapter 5), then this can
be fed into the discussions as they proceed. Again, an outsider is
essential for facilitating such a process.

The whole group can come together and report back at intervals
and/or at the end of the day, with a written report being put together

afterwards. Such a report will consist simply of the group work, copied for all to read.

Step 4 of Future Search – planning how you get to where you want to be – is best tackled after a gap to digest and assess the desired future, and as a kind of 'homework'. This kind of work often involves discovering details which are not easily available during a single meeting, and is probably best done by the official church council or decision-making body. There is more on Future Search and several other large group methods, including Open Space Technology, in the book by Loren B. Mead and Billie T. Alban, *Creating the Future Together.*

The shared management of change

In the last section I emphasized the importance of involving as many people as possible – on a voluntary basis – in the decision making which leads to planned change. By speaking now about the shared management of change, I want to point to something beyond decision making, which still involves a good number of people within a local church. It amounts in fact to the active participation in the practical wisdom of the congregation and the negotiations involved in the development of that wisdom.

The kind of issues that call for major decisions are obvious ones; the day-to-day development of our practical wisdom is also important but usually much less obvious. A metaphor may help: I understand that scientists who study the way our minds and bodies work have discovered that the process involved in hand–eye coordination – as when we reach out to pick up a pencil, for example – involves a whole series of rapid adjustments. Our eyes provide information about where our hand has to go (feedback), and so it starts to move in the general direction of the pencil; as it gets nearer, our eyes provide more precise feedback and our hand movement adjusts accordingly. This all happens so quickly and naturally that we are unaware of the rapid sequence of feedback-adjustment-feedback-adjustment involved. The experience of driving a car provides perhaps a clearer example: we make a familiar journey but the actual driving is never automatic because it involves a sequence of feedback-adjustments whereby we avoid parked cars, allow for other vehicles, stop at red lights, slow down for children crossing, and so on.

Undertaking a review

The practical wisdom that guides us through everyday life as a local church can benefit from a similar pattern of feedback-adjustment, but

Open Space Technology for local churches

Open Space Technology is a wonderful way of involving everyone and generating valuable suggestions. It was discovered by Harrison Owen, a Texan Episcopal priest, in the late 1980s. He found that the part of formal conferences that people most valued turned out to be the coffee breaks! So he set about devising a pattern of meeting that enabled the kind of encounters that happen in coffee breaks to be the dominant feature; you only talk about what really interests you, and you are free to move about and change groups.

The pattern for a local church congregation is fairly simple. You need someone to hold the space for you – a facilitator, someone preferably from outside the congregation itself. The participants ideally sit in a single circle (no front or back row!), and during a brief introduction are invited to write on a card a short statement or question about something they feel strongly about, related to the general theme. (Themes I personally have been involved with include arrangements for a vacancy – the gap between ordained ministers in a congregation – and suggestions for development.) These cards are then sorted – often several people raise essentially the same point – and each topic is allocated a time and a space. Forty-minute sessions work well; the spaces depend on the meeting place.

The 'owner' of the suggestion undertakes to introduce the subject and make notes of the discussion in such a way that this can be reported back to the whole meeting. Participants go to the group discussion that interests them most. The 'law of two feet' applies; you can leave a group at any time, either as a bee, going to pollinate another group with an idea or suggestion you have just heard, or as a butterfly flitting from group to group. The reports can be displayed if they have been written on a flip chart or may be typed up into a document for all to read. They will contain a range of ideas and suggestions – some of which can be put into practice without further ado, some of which may need careful deliberation by the church council.

It may sound chaotic, a meeting without a prearranged agenda and with no prepared input, but it generates a great deal of enthusiasm, ideas and satisfaction. I think a local church could usefully use Open Space as a general review of where it is every year or two; it is certainly a lot more rewarding than the average annual meeting. You will find much more information at <www.openspaceworld.org> and in *Open Space Technology: A User's Guide* by Harrison Owen.

because this wisdom is shared, the process works best when it is made explicit. A periodic review of how we do things can be very productive. It is best undertaken in a spirit of cooperation and mutual support for finding ways of improving what we do, not as a way of simply criticizing present procedures. A large group method like Open Space Technology is well suited to this kind of task.

The fruit of such an exercise can take many forms. Some visible ones are rather like tidying up – a better way of keeping the hymn books, a more efficient system for controlling cash flow, someone moved to donate exhibition boards and so on. But the invisible fruits may be even more important: members feeling that their opinion was valued, an increased ownership of the local church's common life, misunderstandings and misconceptions resolved, a greater willingness to work with each other.

Testing different wisdoms

All these suggested ways of exploring the five areas we have looked at in this chapter embody important insights about the nature of learning, especially the kind of learning appropriate to congregations. Wisdom is first learned as a tradition that is handed down from one generation to another. We grow up in families, communities, schools and local churches that already have a way of doing things which we imitate and incorporate into our own behaviour. Most of this happens unconsciously, not as the result of any organized teaching.

When we move into a new community – a new school, a new place of work, a new family (as happens when people marry) or a new local church – we take a while to learn the new ways of working, the wisdom that holds sway. For many individuals it is a testing time: the new teacher is much stricter than the last one, mother-in-law is not like your own mum, in this church the minister seems to do everything. You can inadvertently step out of line and discover that behaviour that was accepted in the old place is out of order in the new. Even what seem to you helpful suggestions can be received as critical comments which are resented. What may not be so often recognized is that receiving newcomers is a testing time for the host community. The testing is mutual: different wisdoms come up against one another and the proximity can be uncomfortable for both.

An unthinking, unreflective wisdom takes itself for granted, and assumes that its way of life is normal and probably best. Coming up against an alternative way of life presents us with a challenge which makes many people uneasy. It is one thing to learn new information, something you never knew before; it is quite another to be challenged by an alternative way of doing things, especially things you thought you were doing quite normally all along!

Wisdom learns best in such encounters through a process of negotiation. An aggressive response to a rival wisdom is a refusal to learn. It senses that a wisdom, a way of life, is also an embodiment of power, and that to change is to lose, to be defeated.

Wisdom, love and a gospel embodied in a Christian community

I have been involved in education and training for a good long while. When I set out I think I took it for granted that my responsibility was to teach other people important things about the Bible, the Church and life in general, sharing with them what I already knew and had to some extent already mastered myself. But the more I pursued that route, the less satisfactory I found it. For one thing, other people were not always that interested in all the fascinating things that I had learned! For another there were those elusive matters, like love and communion and the fruits of the spirit, which were much more important than all the learned information I had stored in my head. But how do you teach such things?

For some time I had a responsibility for training clergy, and that seemed a strategic activity: train the leaders and everything else would follow. For a while I was particularly encouraged by others to develop collaborative ministry; it was a watchword I was happy to respond to. But in the end I felt that it was much more radical than all of us at first thought. We were in danger of training people one at a time to work together, which was paradoxical. Moreover it was clear to me that many people (myself included) were not natural collaborators in every situation; if I worked well with others in one place there was no guarantee that I would work well in a different one!

When I reflected on what was involved in building up the body of Christ it dawned on me that this was essentially a corporate and shared undertaking. And so I felt I should change the focus of my attention away from clergy and on to the congregation. That shift has enabled me to see and experience quite a number of things differently.

One is that the Christian gospel is communicated not so much by a teacher or preacher as by a community, by the shared witness of people whose following of Jesus Christ is evident in the way they live as much as in what they teach.

Another is that the quality of our shared life of faith as a congregation is affected a great deal by the way we *organize* our common life. This has not received the attention it deserves, partly because many people feel it belongs to the alien world of management rather than to the wisdom of practical theology.

The notion of wisdom is very rich and versatile, holding together practices, knowledge, insight, skill and an openness to learning, as well as having deep roots in Bible, theology and philosophy. It also develops as it is appreciated and reflected on together. Wisdom, as I have already said, is negotiated, which implies that the wise congregation takes responsibility for the development of its own wisdom.

A different discovery I have made as a teacher and trainer is that working in this kind of way with congregations rather than with individuals has been far and away the most rewarding experience. I have enjoyed teaching the Bible, preaching, and Christian ethics, but cooperating with a local church to develop its unique witness to the love of God has been much more exciting.

These insights and others too I have endeavoured to weave into the fabric of this book. It represents no more than a work in progress, a report on where I have got to so far. I hope that those of you who have read it to the end will find it a helpful stimulus to explore a rich and important area for yourselves, and so collaborate in building up the body of Christ.

★★★

The development of our wisdom, Lord,
seems to be closely related to the choices we make
in response to the questions you ask of us.

When we think about it, Jesus asked a lot of questions
which were not designed to elicit information
but rather self-awareness,
and to provoke life-giving choices:
Did you not know that I was bound to be in my Father's house?
Do you want to be healed?
Is it easier to say 'Your sins are forgiven you' or to say 'Stand up and walk'?
Is it permitted to do good or to do evil on the Sabbath?
If you do good only to those who do good to you, what credit is there in that?
Why do you call me 'Lord, Lord' – and never do what I tell you?
Who touched me?

What might such questions be like today?
Are you telling your story – to yourselves as well as to others – in a life-giving, gospel way?

Can you see that your excellent purposes are not the only ones
   worthy of the Lord?
Might God also value an outlook which is quite different from
   yours?

For unique local churches,
the decisive questions will be unique and local too.
But tied up inextricably with the practical questions
about planting new churches or closing some old ones,
about sharing ordained ministers and making drastic cuts,
are other questions about our maturity, our faithfulness,
our desire for love and communion and for the fruits of the spirit.

Lord, help us to respond to today's challenges
in ways which are wise
not just because they are imaginative and realistic
but because they also build up the body of Christ
in the very way they are made.

Further reading

A valuable book for further reading about congregations is Malcolm Grundy, *Understanding Congregations* (London: Mowbray, 1998).

Two books which provide lots of useful information for the study of congregations (though more from the standpoint of an observer than as a way of improving the congregation's own self-awareness) are Helen Cameron et al. (eds), *Studying Local Churches: A Handbook* (London: SCM Press, 2005) and Nancy T. Ammerman et al. (eds), *Studying Congregations: A New Handbook* (Nashville, TN: Abingdon Press, 1998).

A major resource for the study and understanding of congregations is the American *Alban Institute*. Their website is <www.alban.org>. They have published numerous books about many aspects of congregations, including Martin F. Saarinen, *The Life Cycle of a Congregation*, available as a download only from the Alban Institute website.

A classic book about congregations, and one that has influenced me a lot, is James F. Hopewell, *Congregation, Stories and Structures* (Philadelphia, PA: Fortress Press, 1987).

A book which helped change my whole perspective on what is involved in training and learning is Nancy M. Dixon, *The Organizational Learning Cycle: How We Can Learn Collectively* (London: McGraw-Hill, 1994).

A key resource for the development of local churches – which actually provides ways of asking what people think and feel – is provided by Loren B. Mead and Billie T. Alban, *Creating the Future Together: Methods to Inspire Your Whole Faith Community* (Herndon, VA: Alban Institute, 2008). The book itself may not provide all you might need to know in order to use these new methods, but it will point you clearly to further resources. My own favourite is by Harrison Owen, *Open Space Technology: A User's Guide* (San Francisco, CA: Berrett-Koehler, 2008).

Other books referred to in the text:

Penny Edgell Becker, *Congregations in Conflict: Cultural Models of Local Religious Life* (Cambridge: Cambridge University Press, 1999).

R. Meredith Belbin, *Team Roles at Work* (Oxford: Butterworth Heinemann, 1996).

John L. Bell, *The Singing Thing: A Case for Congregational Song* (Glasgow: Wild Goose, 2000).

Hans Frör, *You Wretched Corinthians! The Correspondence between the Church in Corinth and Paul* (London: SCM Press, 1995).

Charles Handy, *Understanding Voluntary Organizations* (London: Penguin, 1988).

David Runcorn, *Spirituality Workbook: A Guide for Explorers, Pilgrims and Seekers* (London: SPCK, 2006).

C. Peter Wagner, *Your Church Can Grow* (Glendale, CA: Regal Books, 1976).

Index